Treehab

LIVING OUT

Gay and Lesbian Autobiographies

David Bergman, Joan Larkin, and Raphael Kadushin
SERIES EDITORS

TREEHAB

Tales

from My Natural, Wild Life

Bob Smith

The University of Wisconsin Press

The University of Wisconsin Press
1930 Monroe Street, 3rd Floor
Madison, Wisconsin 53711-2059
uwpress.wisc.edu

3 Henrietta Street, Covent Garden
London WC2E 8LU, United Kingdom
eurospanbookstore.com

Printed in the United States of America

This book may be available in a digital edition.

Library of Congress Cataloging-in-Publication Data
Names: Smith, Bob, 1958– author.
Title: Treehab: tales from my natural, wild life / Bob Smith.
Other titles: Living out.
Description: Madison, Wisconsin: The University of Wisconsin Press, [2016]
| Series: Living out: gay and lesbian autobiographies
Identifiers: LCCN 2016012945 | ISBN 9780299310509 (cloth: alk. paper)
Subjects: LCSH: Smith, Bob, 1958– | Comedians—United States—Biography.
| Gay men—United States—Biography.
Classification: LCC PN2287.S58 A3 2016 | DDC 792.702/8092 [B] —dc23
LC record available at https://lccn.loc.gov/2016012945

"Walking My Dog through the Valley of the Shadow of Death Is a Nice Way to Start the Day" was originally published in *I'm Not the Biggest Bitch in This Relationship: Hilarious, Heartwarming Tales about Man's Best Friend from America's Favorite Humorists*, edited by Wade Rouse, copyright © 2011 (New York: New American Library, 2011). "Silence = Death: The Education of a Comedian" was originally published in *Love, Christopher Street: Reflections of New York City*, edited by Thomas Keith (New York: Vantage Point, 2012). Both essays are reprinted by permission.

To my Nature Boys:

John Arnold

Michael Hart

Eddie Sarfaty

Michael Zam

Contents

Treehab

Treehab

My partner, Michael Zam, and I had just climbed into bed and pulled up the comforter. We'd driven three hours northeast of Toronto to Little Straggle Lake and were staying in Elvira Kurt and Chloë Brushwood Rose's cottage, which they've named "Treehab," a joke of Elvira's that I not only love but also wish I'd thought of myself. It was the end of August and the night was chilly. Summers in the far north remind you—even on the hottest days—that the sun is a fire in the sky: when it goes out, the room grows cold. Before turning off the light, we overheard three-year-old Madeline having a conversation in the bedroom next to ours.

"Are Bob and Michael boys?" Her sweet babyish voice sounded as if she was inquiring about the gender of the Easter bunny.

"Yes, honey," Elvira replied. "They're boys."

Michael and I chuckled quietly. "I'm glad she cleared that up," Michael whispered.

I said, "Maybe Maddie's confused because we're not as butch as some of her moms' lesbian friends."

"Speak for yourself."

This was Michael's first visit to see Maddie. We had flown from New York City to Buffalo to stay with my mother and then headed to Toronto. Madeline had instantly taken to Michael, grabbing him by the hand. "Michael! Hurry! Come inside my house!" He obeyed, promptly entering her "house," an area near the sofa where her toy stove stood. "Bob! You too!" Madeline was at the delightful age where she sounded exactly like a children's book: speaking in short declarative sentences that ended in exclamation points. It's probably the only time in our lives when conversation naturally emulates literature.

Treehab is located in Harcourt Park, a 6,900-acre cottage commune near Algonquin Provincial Park. Harcourt Park has eighteen lakes, but only eight lakes have cottages, and the rest of the land will never be developed. As soon as we arrived at Treehab, Elvira and I took Maddie for a canoe ride. Michael dove in the water and swam beside us. We stopped in a swampy part of the lake, where Maddie and I hunted for frogs among the reeds. We caught a small green frog, which Maddie held in her palm for a second and then released.

Her elation reminded me of the start of my fairy tale. I've loved the wild since I was a five-year-old and went camping with my family in the Adirondacks. I was given a pagan welcome to the woods while running in the forest at night with my brothers and sister. Tripping over a log, I tumbled to the ground and then stood up and realized something was squirming in the front pocket of my shorts. I reached in and felt something alive. It was a toad. It didn't disgust me; it thrilled me. My one regret was not kissing my toad, since it might have been my first prince. I'd always tried to capture frogs and toads and knew instinctively that one seeking me out was a hug from the wild.

Four years before Michael's introduction to Maddie, Elvira and Chloë had asked me to be their sperm donor. I was surprised and flattered, and it made me understand why so many straight men are insufferably cocksure. A big part of the appeal of heterosexuality is that every act of sexual intercourse holds out the possibility of reproduction: the condom could break, the diaphragm could leak, or the pill could be a placebo. Therefore, having sex with a woman is a pat on the back of every man's penis—even for men whose DNA should be thought of as an abbreviation for "Do Not Approach."

A few years before she met Chloë, Elvira had discussed having a baby with me.

"I want to do it the natural way. I think we'll only need to do it once." Then the comedian in her added, "Believe me, we'll only want to do it once." We both laughed. Elvira and I have been friends for many years. We first met when we performed stand-up together in Toronto and became close when we lived together for two weeks in Sydney. We were performing at a queer comedy festival, and the performers lived in a lavish residential-style hotel where each room was a two-bedroom suite. When we arrived in Australia, the festival's producer told Elvira and me, "I've put the boys with boys and girls with girls except for you two. Somehow I know you'll get along." She was right. We were predisposed to becoming friends since we each thought the other was funny. It's impossible for a hilarious comedian to become close friends with a comedian who isn't; it's like a vegan falling in love with a butcher.

Before Elvira brought up the subject, I'd never really seriously considered reproducing. At least that's what I'd always believed until recently. Eight years ago, I moved from Santa Fe to New York and, while going through some files, found the proposal for my second book of comic essays. It was written in 1998, long before Elvira mentioned becoming her donor and when I was still with my ex, Tom:

On Being a Father—Our friends Judy and Sharon recently had a baby, and our friends Nanette and Tommy have just had their second child, so Tom and I have officially become Gay Uncles. I would love to write about the possibility of becoming a father because to my astonishment, I actually think I would make a good one.

I'd forgotten I'd written this. Rereading it reminded me how much I'd changed since I first came out in the early eighties. Back then I presumed that my being gay precluded having children. In fact, I thought of it as one of the advantages of my sexual orientation. My friends and I never talked about children unless a baby was crying on an airplane. Most of us were aspiring bohemians, and artists feel overwhelmed providing day care for their inner child—let alone nurturing a real kid.

Back then, I had one gay friend who had a daughter, but he was considered an understandable anomaly because Gary was in his early forties—most of us were in our twenties—and he had once been married to a woman. His daughter was a souvenir from his trip to heterosexuality.

But the Reagan era was a time when gay men and lesbians realized that our government and much of the culture didn't care whether we died of AIDS. Their enmity actually did gay people a favor since when people are rooting for your death they immediately lose any influence over your life. They didn't want us to join the military, get married, or have children. And since reproduction is the simplest do-it-with-some-one-else project, many of us started families.

In the midnineties, Sharon Callahan and Judy Gold, two of my closest friends, wanted to start a family. They decided that Sharon would have their first child and Judy their second. They briefly discussed having my ex Tom or me as a donor. During the conversation Judy—another comic—said, "Let's see, Tom's good looking but can't decide on a career, and Bob's smart but his father was an alcoholic. Great!"

Lesbians can afford to be ruthlessly discriminating when picking a sperm donor. In fact if all women were as selective as lesbians, we'd have evolved into a race of gods by now. Like most of us, my family has genetic pluses and minuses. My dad died of alcoholism, and my mother and sister both suffered from depression, which makes me think of my DNA as a make-it-a-double helix. On the plus side, I've never been prone to depression, I've tried to keep my booze and pot intake recreational instead of vocational, and I'm smart, funny, and handsome—though when I look back at photos of myself in my late twenties, I find it hard to believe I never thought I was. I'm not being conceited because there is one thing I do know: if you can't admit your virtues after forty, you won't make it to fifty. Our biggest drawback as donors for Judy and

Sharon was that Tom and I were goys; they wanted a Jewish donor and didn't buy my argument that every successful stand-up comedian should be considered part Jewish. There were no hard feelings on my part when Sharon chose an anonymous Jewish donor. I knew Judy well enough to know that the child would be *their* son except when he did something wrong; then he'd be *mine*. My contribution of a Y chromosome would allow her to yell an accusatory "WHY?" in my direction every time our child did something she disliked.

It took Sharon almost two years to get pregnant. Sometimes after she went to the doctor to get inseminated, I'd suggest the two of us should lie in bed and smoke cigarettes in order to increase the chances of her getting knocked up. Sharon eventually gave birth to Henry. I became his "Uncle Bob," and the two of us developed a rapport almost immediately. I'm not exactly sure what it was he liked about me, although I always answered his questions without talking down to him. This wasn't a conscious strategy to win Henry's affection. Rather it was more of a response to my own childhood experiences. I resented being treated as a child and fondly recalled the occasions when I'd been treated like an adult. When I was in the fifth grade, I loved that my grandmother would always bring me the previous week's copy of *Newsweek* because she knew I followed current affairs—cheering on the Czechs when the Russians invaded in 1968.

When Henry was very young, we took him to Disneyland, and he insisted on sitting next to me on all the rides. As we were leaving a restaurant one night, Sharon said, "Henry, you need to put on your jacket." He twisted up his face into a small fist of protest. Sharon shot me a conspiratorial look. "Uncle Bob is wearing his jacket," she said. Henry looked up at me and without another word put on his jacket. Sharon leaned over to me, "Isn't it nice that someone idolizes you?" "Nice" hardly did justice to the bliss I felt.

It was entirely gratifying because children's affection is straightforward. There's no underlying agenda of sucking up to you because you can advance a child's career selling lemonade or boost his reputation by

attending his next show-and-tell presentation. Henry liked me because
he liked me. And I liked him. He was curious about everything and
cracked jokes almost from the time he began talking. Henry had always
been able to talk about his feelings, which made me feel I could also talk
about mine. When I took Henry to the museum of natural history, I
could say, "Look, we all want to have fun today, so as soon as you've
had enough, tell me."

After Henry's brother, Ben, was born, when I'd take them to the
playground, I'd say, "No fighting or crying." And for the most part,
there wasn't any fighting or crying. I know that encouraging boys to
suppress their feelings could be considered psychologically unhealthy.
But from my experience, men whose emotions are stunted can learn
later to express their feelings, while men whose every emotion is un-
bridled end up as either unbearable queens or psychotic dictators whose
every murderous impulse is acted upon.

Henry and I don't share the same interests in everything. He loves
basketball, and it made me laugh when after we played he told his
mothers, "Uncle Bob's terrible at basketball." It wasn't said maliciously
but more as a statement of fact, which made his mothers and me laugh
even harder.

My relationship with Henry profoundly changed how I thought
about children. The first time I babysat for him, I brought the *New
York Times*, assuming that I'd read the paper while he played a game or
watched television. No. Henry insisted that I play with him for the entire
time—for five hours. When Judy returned from her television taping, I
admitted, "I don't know if I could do this full time."

"Now you know why I'm exhausted all the time," Judy said.

"How did our mothers do it?" My mother had four children and
Judy's had three.

"With Librium," Judy said, naming a tranquilizer popular in the
sixties. "I'd be drinking vodka gimlets for breakfast if I had four kids."

After spending the morning with Henry, it was clear that I wouldn't
enjoy being a full-time parent.

About a year after Elvira met Chloë, the two of them asked me to be their sperm donor. It was a momentous occasion, but unfortunately Hallmark hasn't produced any greeting cards to mark this special event:

> Roses are red,
> Sunflowers are huge,
> Stay out of our bed,
> We just want your splooge.

I said yes and they were ready to begin baby making ASAP, which suddenly gave me qualms. I barely knew Chloë; I'd liked her immediately, but then every gay man has a history of meeting guys you like immediately whom you don't like later. It was awkward to admit that I needed more time; I wanted to get to know Chloë better and feel as close to her as I did to Elvira. I also wanted to be clear about exactly what our roles would be. Soon after, Chloë and Elvira visited me in Los Angeles, where we talked about everything, and then I visited them in Toronto. During several months of discussions, we agreed they would be the parents and I would be the funcle. The baby would know I was her/his biological father, but I would be the baby's Bob. We discussed what would happen if the two of them split up, and they assured me that I would always be a part of the baby's life. My reasoning was that since I trusted Elvira and Chloë to raise our baby, I could trust that they weren't going to screw me—literally or figuratively. For me, this was an emotional commitment among all of us, a commitment that would last our lifetimes. While we weren't starting a family, we were choosing to become Family.

The more time I spent with Chloë, the more I grew to love her: she's a super-smart bookworm, has a great sense of humor, makes delicious meals, and even though she's younger than Elvira and me, she's more mature than either of us. When I finally said, "Yes. Let's do it," I had no doubt that it was the right decision; I looked forward to spending time with Elvira and Chloë for the rest of my life.

Before we tried to have a baby, I needed to be tested for sexually transmitted diseases and also needed to have a sperm count done. In California, you can't have a lab do a sperm count without a doctor's prescription, and I was warned not to mention my homosexuality since many labs refuse to test gay men. Fortunately, a friend of mine, Jay, had just graduated from medical school. When I told him my problem, he wrote me a prescription. Jay was gay and actually got a kick out of screwing the homophobic medical system. When I went for my sperm test, the jerk-off room had several issues of *Hustler* magazine, which made me think less of the straight donors and made me wish I'd brought an issue of gay porn to leave as reading material. My test results were fine; it turned out my boys could swim and I had no STDs. We were ready to go.

My first donation took place at my house in Los Angeles. No doctor was involved as the gals had thoroughly researched how to make a baby without fucking. In some ways it felt like we were doing a science fair project. I went into my bedroom and masturbated into a disposable, clear plastic cup. Part of me wondered if the kid would come out looking like the guy I fantasized about. After a short time I came out of my room bearing a hot cup of Joe or Josephine. Elvira came out of their room, grabbed the cup, thanked me, returned to their room, and closed the door. It was definitely awkward for all of us, but none of us commented on it until weeks later in Toronto when my jerking off into a cup twice a day had become a household chore. I realized that we might have become too comfortable on the day I brought my cup upstairs while Chloë was on the telephone. When she saw me, she said to whomever she was speaking, "I'm sorry, I've got to go. Bob and I are inseminating this morning." I suggested her declaration would be the perfect way to fend off unwanted phone solicitations.

While we were trying to get pregnant, I told my mother that Elvira and Chloë had asked me to be their donor. I braced myself for a negative reaction, but my mother's response wasn't critical. She asked me how raising the child would work and if I'd thought carefully about all the ramifications. Her questions were thoughtful and practical. She'd met Elvira and Chloë and had immediately liked them. After I explained what my role would be—deadbeat donor—she gave her blessing, "All right." Then she said as an afterthought, "Children are wonderful, but you're opening yourself up to the possibility of great pain." She looked at me intently, making me think that she was referring to my sister Carol's suicide. Her comment made me reflect on how courageous it is to have a child. Unconditional love also holds out the threat of unconditional pain. Her comment wasn't meant to shake my resolve but was more of a reflection on how much both my mother and I missed my sister.

A few weeks later, my mother called and I told her I was packing for a flight to Toronto.

"For the miracle?" she asked, which made both of us laugh.

When Chloë and Elvira called to tell me we were pregnant, I experienced the thrilling elation that's always portrayed in television shows and movies as a moment of rapturous joy. And it is. It was one of those moments where you remember exactly where you were when you heard the news. I was in a 1960s-vintage motel room with my friends and colleagues in Key West in a show called Funny Gay Males. When I broke the news to them, one of the Males, Danny, responded, "Oh, Mrs. Smith, you're going to be a mother!"

Chloë was six months pregnant when she and Elvira were married in Toronto. I was their best man and was horribly tempted, as comedians often are, to introduce myself with a joke to their family and friends. "Hi, I'm Bob," I imagined myself saying. "I'm the best man who knocked up one of the brides."

When it got closer to the baby's due date, we discussed the actual birth. Chloë and Elvira wanted the birth to be an intimate event between the two of them and asked nicely if I would wait to visit the baby after he or she was born. Their request seemed reasonable to me; I didn't mind not being at the baby's birth because I hadn't been at the conception either.

Chloë and Elvira were convinced the baby was a boy while I had no doubt she was a girl. I can't explain my certainty other than a gut feeling that after my sister's death, which had been devastating for me, another woman would enter my life. My conviction wasn't based upon a belief in reincarnation. It was based upon a belief in symmetry; an important woman had left my life, and the universe owed me one.

I wanted Chloë and Elvira to feel that the baby was theirs, although I did insist on being the first person they called after the baby was born.

Speaking in a low voice, Elvira called and left me a message on November 25 announcing the birth of Madeline Inez Brushwood Kurt. She was in Chloë's hospital room, trying not to wake her. I've received several birth announcement calls, and the caller's voice is always suffused with the unmistakable sound of incredulity and relief. Every sentence sounds like it's punctuated with a question mark. Listening to the message, I realized how relieved I was by the news. You avoid thinking about all the horrible things that could go wrong, but those fears can't be shaken until the baby makes an actual appearance. During her pregnancy Chloë had preeclampsia, and her health was as much a concern for us as the baby's.

I immediately called my mother. "Oh, that's wonderful!" she said.

Meeting Madeline for the first time, I wondered if I'd feel some special connection with her and worried that perhaps I wouldn't. We met when she was one month old. I'd already seen photographs of her and was relieved that she looked cute. (Other less partial observers told me they thought she did also.) Shortly after I arrived, Madeline fell asleep in my arms. While I lay on the couch for two hours, she slept on my stomach, and all the tender feelings of love I hoped would appear did.

From the start, Maddie has been wildly enthusiastic about being alive; her first word was "Wow!" (I'm still not certain this wasn't part of an incomplete exclamation, "Wow! All three of you are queer?") Every time I see Maddie, I observe new aspects of her: her love of drawing with watercolor markers, her excitement when holding a tiny frog in her palm, her telling me that she wants to paddle the canoe, and then her instantaneous discovery that it's much better to be a passenger as she handed me the oar. People are always asking me, "Does she resemble you?" Physically she doesn't. She has blue eyes and blonde hair, but her love of frogs is mine and so, unfortunately, is her desire to have someone else paddle.

One of the unexpected bonuses of becoming a deadbeat donor is that it became a new source of material for my stand-up act. People always assume that comedians do everything for material, but in my case it honestly didn't occur to me. But then I'd make a remark to my friend Eddie Sarfaty such as "I love that there are gay parents now. Twenty-five years ago, did anyone ever think that one day bottles of poppers and lube would need childproof caps?" He laughed, and then I thought it was so wrong to think that—let alone say it. But of course, I've said that onstage, and it's gotten a big laugh. And then I added, "That's so wrong for me to be saying that." And that also gets a laugh.

After Madeline was born, my mother naturally wanted Chloë and Elvira's address in Toronto to send a gift for the baby. A dress and card were sent, followed a month later by Christmas presents and a card. Then a New Year's card, and Valentine's Day, St. Patrick's Day, and Easter cards—basically every holiday except for Arbor Day and Lincoln's birthday.

It soon became apparent to all of us that while I wasn't going to be Madeline's dad, my mother was going to be one of her grandmothers. This concerned me because I hadn't discussed it with Elvira and Chloë. It was logical because my mother had no other grandchildren, and she'd mentioned to me several times in the past that she hated that. "All the girls in card club talk about their grandchildren," she said enviously. "I'm sick of it." For almost forty years my mother has played pinochle with the same group of women, and my mother was the only one without grandchildren. Chloë and Elvira quickly dispelled any concerns I had that my mother might be infringing upon them. They immediately dubbed my mother "Grandma Sue." A trade imbalance of baby clothes from Buffalo soon followed.

My mother's unconditional love for Madeline gratified me. And her love was clearly unconditional because at Madeline's first birthday party, we heard that Maddie was using her tiny fingernails like a velociraptor, scratching kids at her day care. My mother laughed approvingly. "She's a pistol!" Later when Maddie swatted me and cut my upper lip, my mother appeared to be delighted. "She won't take anything from anyone!" When I checked my gashed lip in a mirror, I realized I wasn't upset either. I loved that at the age of one, Maddie already displayed the attitude of a tough biker chick wielding a switchblade: "Don't fuck with me or I'll cut you!" My response reminded me of my father's when in the eighth grade I was suspended for three days for fighting. My dad was more pleased than upset when he heard the news.

Elvira and Chloë decided they wanted a brother or sister for Maddie, and they asked me for another donation. Our son, Xander, was born when Maddie was four.

Giving my mother grandchildren has given me a leg up in my mother's esteem. And I'm also not above using them to get my way with her. Before an election I always worry that my Republican brothers will sway my mother to vote for their repulsive candidates, so I use my trump card. I remind my mother that the Republicans are antigay. "You know, Mom, if Madeline and Xander lived here, the Republicans would be against their parents." And I'll add, "They're also antienvironmental. So your grandchildren will inherit a shitty planet." It thrills and amuses me when my mother responds, "Those bastards!"

I've always been an environmentalist, and I want my children to enjoy a beautiful world, so global warming isn't an impersonal issue for me. If you're a parent voting for antienvironmental, climate-change-denying idiots who don't conserve anything, then child protective services should put your kids in foster care, since it's clear you don't care about their welfare. I definitely want to teach Maddie and Xander that being angry about other people's selfishness and lack of compassion is actually a virtue.

I don't dwell on the hardships or dangers Madeline and Xander might face—or the sorrow they might experience—because I'm consumed with the more distressing anxiety that I might be the one to hurt them. About a year after Madeline was born, I was diagnosed with ALS/ Lou Gehrig's disease. (I don't have familial ALS, I have the sporadic version, so Maddie and Xander won't inherit this fucking illness.) While I worry about my health, I also worry about my children. I'm afraid I'll die before they are old enough to know—or even remember—me, and I'm immodest enough to think that people who don't know me are missing out on something terrific. During the last ten years, Maddie and Xander have seen me lose my voice; it has made Maddie cry since she thinks I'm dying. I don't want them to remember me for this fucking disease.

There are so many things I want to share with Maddie and Xander; for example, how marvelous it is that they are Canadian. My father was born in Canada, and they come from a long line; they're eighth- or ninth-generation Canadian. Their direct ancestor Nicholas Smith fought with Butler's Rangers and the Iroquois against the Americans during the Revolution, something I never learned until my midforties. My grandfather lived in Buffalo for his entire adult life but always proudly referred to himself as a Canadian. (He would watch the late-night American news and also the Canadian news, which seemed strange to me as a child because in the pre-cable days, television reception from Canada was a blur of snow. I now think that was strangely apropos.) It's amusing to think that being American was a one-generation aberration.

I'm not worried that Maddie and Xander will be bereft of wise counsel since their parents, Elvira and Chloë, are two of the smartest, most loving, and thoughtful people I know. Of course, it's hard not to wonder while I'm writing this if Maddie and Xander will be reading it when I'm dead. (Hi, Maddie! Hi, Xander!) Books have been vastly important in my life—as both a reader and a writer. I've learned that the great gift of literature is that someone else's tale becomes a chapter of your story. And I still feel books are the best art form for making contact with another consciousness, which is why reading a good book by yourself never feels lonely. But I don't want Maddie and Xander to know me only through my books.

I also have a small store of wisdom I'd like to impart to them: my belief that it's okay to be skeptical but never to be cynical; and my one litmus test for all religions—never believe in a god who's meaner than you are. (And I'm limiting the "you" in that sentence to Maddie, Xander, and myself because you—the reader—could be a nasty nutjob.) My most important piece of advice would be to have fun, something Maddie and Xander already understand instinctively.

On our last day at Treehab when Michael first met Maddie, the four grown-ups were sitting at the picnic table drinking coffee while Maddie was drawing on the deck with bright-colored chalks. She drew a green frog surrounded by magenta daisies. Next she drew two stick figures holding hands. "This is Bob and Michael!" she shouted. One figure was cobalt blue, and the other one was rose colored.

"Bob's the pink guy," Michael declared, making the four adults laugh.

The deck was an island of sunshine surrounded by a dark tangle of trees. There were neighboring cabins, but the forest made other people seem like woodpeckers. You could occasionally hear them, but you'd have to search to find them. Sipping coffee in the woods feels like you've found the perfect balance between civilized and wild, an elusive ratio in every life.

Suddenly a loon called out on the lake, a sound that is always called "haunting," but that word has never seemed precise to me. The connotation of haunting is too somber for such an exhilarating cry. (My definition of an asshole would be someone who hears a loon's call and says, "I hope we don't have to hear that racket all night.") Maddie kept drawing, which was fine because she'll have many opportunities to hear a loon, but Michael had never heard a loon before. Then the loon flew over our heads and cried again, something I'd never observed before.

A loon's cry is beautiful and strange. Life is also beautiful and strange. It's strange because we're chalk drawings that will fade away. I want Maddie and Xander to know that their father thinks hearing a loon's yawp is a better sermon than listening to any preacher. That holding a frog is more fun than holding a gun. That sitting at a picnic table in the sunshine in the woods with people you love is better than any fancy dinner with millionaires. And they'll know it when they read this book.

My Stone Age

Even as a boy, I never understood the cautionary proverb "Curiosity killed the cat." The trade-off sounds fair to me. The cat's life might have been short, but at least it didn't drag.

My greatest adventure was due to my curiosity about whether I could become a comedian and writer. Most of the time, I've found that my initial curiosity can be satisfied quickly, as a short conversation with an underwear model once proved. But it's marvelous and disturbing to admit that while I steadily develop new interests, I never seem to lose any of my old ones. I still enjoy almost all the things I liked as a boy and teenager: dinosaurs, UFOs, snakes and turtles, Native Americans, wildlife, history, Alaska, Canada, Australia, Russia, archaeology, ancient Greece, ecology, outer space, the Ice Age and Neanderthals, comedy, lost tribes, lost cities and lost civilizations, fossils, rocks and minerals, politics and presidential elections, architecture, art and artists, reading and literature, and Hercules movies. (Alas, I'm no longer interested in Hercules movies, although I'm still fascinated by men who look like demigods.)

Recently I've been thinking about the curiosity of boys. When my son, Xander, was two years old, he was transfixed by toys, pets, spoons, deflated balloons, wagging fingers, crumpled-up balls of aluminum foil, and was fascinated by all people. Everyone. I guess a baby's immune system to boredom also needs time to develop. Xander loved to pick up rocks; he thought they were dinosaur eggs. He also loved Lady Gaga's music and demanded it in the car.

Of course, I don't think curiosity is determined by gender. At the age of five, his sister, Maddie, could tell you which dinosaur skeleton at the Royal Ontario Museum was a Maiasaura. But as an infant, Madeline was more reserved than Xander. Long before she could talk, she had a cool, appraising, blue-eyed stare that asked, "Who the fuck are you? And why are you holding me?"

Xander was just beginning to talk and hadn't started to listen. Once he learned to listen, he had a reason to cry after figuring out how dull and stupid some people can be. At the time, Xander's tender smiles were bestowed upon the world with a largesse that was the essence of innocence. He reminded me that I was also a curious boy and have grown into a curious man.

Not all of my juvenile interests stuck. I loved trains as a little boy and my father would drive me over to the railroad tracks to watch the choo-choos. Trains lose their allure once boys are old enough to understand that locomotives are just a form of transportation, and having a fascination with trains is about as interesting as having a fixation on buses.

I can't remember not being interested in dinosaurs. All parents encourage a love of dinosaurs since the chances of your kid finding a baby triceratops and bringing it home and begging to keep it as a pet are pretty small. By the second grade, I grew warm blooded at the thought of brontosaurs walking the earth. The trouble with being a child is that satisfying your curiosity is dependent on adults. It took weeks of nagging to get my mother to take me to the Buffalo Museum of Science, where she patiently let me look at every fossil exhibit while she puffed her way through a pack of Parliaments.

When I wanted to buy a dinosaur book at the gift shop, she suggested that I borrow one from the public library, which was within walking distance of our house. I borrowed and read three children's books on dinosaurs, a word I learned was Greek for "terrible lizards." Terrible lizards was kind of a letdown. It made a Tyrannosaurus rex sound like an unhousebroken pet being scolded by my mother.

After I finished those books, Miss Momberger, the librarian, kindly suggested that I try the adult section of the library to see what books they had on the subject. Miss Momberger was a tiny, elderly, unmarried woman whom my mother referred to as a spinster, a word that sounded appealingly like beatnik slang to my ear. (I went through a phase where I was enamored of beatnik slang. In the third grade, I said to my teacher, Miss Hill, "Cool it, daddy-o!" In retrospect, she was clearly a butch lesbian, which might explain why she didn't take kindly to my remark.) Miss Momberger led me upstairs to the adult book section, and it felt like a rite of passage. She recommended the first book I ever read that had more print than illustrations. It was called *All About Dinosaurs*, an account of Roy Chapman Andrews's fossil hunting expedition in the 1920s to the Gobi Desert, where the first dinosaur eggs were discovered.

This immediately led me to the belief that fossils could be found anywhere, my reasoning being that the rocks of the Gobi Desert and rocks in the suburbs of Buffalo couldn't be that different. That summer, I started hunting for fossils and made my first find at Allegany State Park. It still sits on a shelf in my living room. It's a piece of shale with three impressions of 250-million-year-old brachiopods, which to the untrained eye look like prehistoric clams.

My interest in fossils led to an interest in rocks, since fossils are basically rocks with a good story to tell. This led me to rock collecting, a pastime for the most elementary of hoarders. As luck would have it, at the time I began to covet minerals, a new business opened on Delaware Avenue, the main street of Kenmore, my hometown. The words "Fimbel's Lapidary Shop" were painted over the door—and then in smaller letters on the window "Rocks and Minerals."

During the time Fimbel's remained in business, I became a frequent visitor and an occasional customer. The proprietor was Bud Fimbel, a tall handsome man in his twenties. He wore a pair of horn-rimmed eyeglasses, and the thick black hair on his arms made them look like shoe brushes. Over the course of eight months, Bud went from entrepreneurial optimism to the harried look of a hobbyist who had lamentably come to understand that his arcane interest would never become a commercially viable business.

Unfortunately, Bud opened his business at the dawning of the Age of Aquarius, fifteen years away from the dawning of the New Age when crystals developed spiritual attributes, and healing chunks of quartz sitting on coffee tables became as indispensable in Manhattan apartments as an air conditioner. In the late 1960s the market for collecting rocks was, as far as I could tell, limited to one boy with an allowance of $1.50 a week and the thirty or so grown men within a hundred miles of Buffalo who delighted in the acquisition of choice ore samples.

When I entered Fimbel's Lapidary for the first time, a small bell on the door jingled, and I now feel that the ringing wasn't announcing the presence of a customer so much as mourning the loss of Bud's life savings. The difference between Fimbel's sparsely stocked store and an empty storefront was negligible. The store looked like an abandoned quarry where the rocks were left in place at the end of the day when the steam whistle blew. Presentation was a concept that eluded Mr. Fimbel, but a stylish showcase for his inventory couldn't be expected from a man whose heart pounded at the sight of a gravel pit. Mr. Fimbel had hung a few shelves and installed two glass display cases, one of which still featured a faded advertisement for another business failure: Hoak's Birch Beer! It was ominous that Mr. Fimbel didn't take the time to remove the advertisement from the display case. There should be a small-business superstition about it being bad luck to have the logo of a failed business on the premises of a new business.

One display case was filled with rocks and minerals, sold in clear plexiglass caskets, each specimen nestled in foam rubber. The other showcased chunky jewelry that was too geologic to appeal to women and yet too feminine to appeal to male rock collectors. On the wall, behind the cash box, Mr. Fimbel had framed the first dollar he'd earned. It was hung in a burst of optimism, but the noncommittal expression on George Washington's face made it look like even he had doubts about the business.

Workbenches, lathes, and grinding tools took up a large part of the store. I had to step around a cairn of rocks once I got past the doorway.

Mr. Fimbel put down his fried-bologna hero and asked, "Is there anything special that you're looking for?" He wasn't a fat man, but every time I came in the store he was eating something: a slice of pizza, a chicken leg, or two foot-long hot dogs.

"Do you have any petrified wood?"

"I sure do," Mr. Fimbel said with a wait-until-you-see-this smile. He went over to one of the shelves and pulled down a dirty half-crumpled shoe box. Inside were several splintered gray-and-brown chunks jumbled into a petrified wood pile. They didn't bear any resemblance to the red, orange, and yellow pieces of petrified wood I had seen at the Museum of Science. Mistaking my disappointment for doubts about their authenticity, he reassured me, "Those are REAL pieces of petrified wood."

I didn't know what to say. I was almost ten years old, mature enough to understand that many adults were bonkers—but too young to feel comfortable expressing my observations to these wackos. You had to look closely at the pieces to determine that they had once been wood. Charcoal briquettes were more exciting. Twigs would have inspired more awe.

"I can give you a good price on any of those." With the slightest hint of pleading, he added, "I will even take 20 percent off my discount."

I had to say something because I was beginning to worry that our duet of commerce would end up with him begging, "Will you please just buy one of these fucking rocks?!"

"Yeah, these are neat," I lied. "What else do you have?"

"Have you ever seen the inside of a geode?"

"No."

"Well, look at this." He pointed to a rubber bucket labeled "crystal geodes." Sitting on top of the pile was one neatly sliced in two. It resembled a prehistoric gumball that somebody bit in half and, disgusted by the artificial grape flavor, had thrown away. Then over thousands of years, the forces of nature transformed sugar and food coloring into amethyst.

"You pick one out, and I'll slice it open for you right now." He sounded like a waiter trying to entice me to order the lobster.

"Are they all the same on the inside?"

"Um, yeah." Trying to put a good spin on that fact, he added, "But each one is unique."

The geodes cost four bucks. That was a lot of money for me back then. They looked okay, but the prize inside a box of Cracker Jacks offered up more suspense.

"Do you have any fossils?"

"You bet I do."

In the showcase, he pointed out an entire row of trilobites: small fossilized arthropods that looked like the ancestor of potato bugs. I wondered if trilobites also rolled up into a ball if you tapped them with a Popsicle stick.

"They look like potato bugs," I said, not having learned yet to sometimes keep my thoughts to myself.

"Well, sort of. But these were ancestors of the potato bug. They're 250 million years old."

If I brought one home, I could imagine my mother saying, "You paid two dollars for an old bug?" And as much as I liked fossils, I had to admit she would have a point.

Mr. Fimbel finally did the sensible thing and said, "Why don't you just look around, and if you have any questions, I'll be happy to answer them. Feel free to open boxes. Just don't mix things up."

Since everything was a heap of rubble, looking for rocks at Fimbel's was closer to beachcombing than shopping. After methodically working my way from agate to rhodium, I decided to leave. When he saw me headed for the door, Mr. Fimbel asked, "Have you ever seen luminescent minerals?"

"Glow in the dark?"

"Yep."

"No."

"Come on back here."

In the back of the shop, he'd built a small partition where six aquariums were shelved. Inside each aquarium were several large rocks. It looked like he had started collecting tropical fish, but they had all died and he decided to just empty the water and enjoy the gravel on the bottom of the tanks.

Mr. Fimbel turned off the light switch in the partition and turned on the lamps over each aquarium. The lamps emitted a violet shadow, and each of the rocks glowed: some hot pink and orange, others a sickly green, others a combination of blue, green, and red. I was impressed. These were rock stars.

"They glow under ultraviolet light," he said.

"They're cool."

It didn't occur to me then that Mr. Fimbel was missing out on a great business opportunity. It was 1967 and psychedelia was in full flower power. He should have been marketing luminescent rocks to college students tripping on acid—not nine-year-old boys.

Next, Mr. Fimbel tried to interest me in his special pursuit: lapidary. Farther back in the store, I heard something rattling in cans. Bud opened a door and showed me four rotating lathes attached to four revolving Chase & Sanborn coffee cans.

"Lapidary is easy and fun. With just some basic equipment, you can polish rough minerals into semiprecious stones!"

"How long does it take?"

"Only two months!"

"That long?"

"It's nothing. Once you get going, the time flies. And the polishing goes on night and day. Before you know it, you'll be making quartz crystals into polished pieces suitable for jewelry. Once you start, there's not much you have to do. If you get more than one coffee can going, then every other week you can be taking stones out."

A hobby based on erosion was too dull—even for me. I preferred rocks in their natural state. The small polished pebbles Mr. Fimbel showed me looked like unappealing candy.

The more he tried to interest me in lapidary, the more drawbacks I could see. Having four machines running continuously in the basement wouldn't go over too well with my father. He hated it when we left the dining room light on or opened the refrigerator door before we had decided what we wanted. He'd yell, "What are you doing? Cooling off the house? Shut the refrigerator door!" The spinning coffee cans would have to produce diamonds from coal, or else my father would never stop complaining about the amount of electricity I was wasting.

I usually visited Fimbel's once a week and eventually bought three rocks after mulling over each purchase for months, as if every decision in my head was a tumbling unpolished stone. First, I bought a piece of asbestos.

"That's a beauty," he said.

The label indicated that it was mined in Quebec. Mineral asbestos is a metallic green with long white filaments giving the rock an almost Rapunzel quality. My second purchase was of a small piece of uranium glass. "It's radioactive!" said Mr. Fimbel. It was a bright chartreuse color and under ultraviolet light became dayglow, like it was trying to shout, "Cancer!"

By some unerring instinct I had picked the two deadliest rocks since the one David chucked at Goliath. I'm not going to be surprised when research reveals early exposure to asbestos and radioactive glass can cause ALS.

My third purchase was a piece of Iceland spar, a transparent rhomboid-shaped piece of calcite that is double refracting. It cost three dollars—two weeks' allowance—but I loved it. When the Iceland spar was placed over handwriting, the letters appeared doubled. It was almost as if I had an inkling that I would need something to make reading prescriptions for ALS more fun.

☙

Fimbel's Lapidary Shop went out of business overnight. There was a big Closed sign in the window, and all the rocks were cleared out. But I kept my deadly collection for years in my dresser, ignorant that I was probably the last person in America to install asbestos in his house.

When I was nine, I asked for a junior geologist's set for Christmas. It came with fifteen bottles of chemicals and twenty small sample rocks and minerals—in case the buyer was unsure of what a rock looked like. It also included an alcohol lamp that you could sprinkle powdered iron pyrite into to create sparks. Best of all, the set came with a child-sized miner's pick and a small vial of hydrochloric acid. Giving a nine-year-old boy a vial of acid and a pick hammer was like giving a six-pack and set of car keys to a sixteen-year-old. The junior geologist was supposed to place a drop of acid on a rock sample, and by observing the reaction, he or she could determine its identity. But I never felt the need to distinguish whether feldspar was a rock or a mineral. There were better uses for my acid.

Small boys worship Kali the destroyer and show their devotion by breaking off five of the arms on her statue. In the spirit of scientific inquiry, I used the acid to burn holes in paper, crayons, potato chips, and a strand of my sister's hair. The course of my scientific investigations led me, like Galileo and Darwin, into controversy about my methods. My sister didn't appreciate it when I used my acid to burn a hole in her Barbie doll, and she started screaming when Barbie's smile became an oozing cold sore. My mother's explosive chemical reaction furthered my awareness that she wasn't made of money and that I didn't respect other people's property.

All of my odd interests came into focus at a very early age, when my aunt Ann, my favorite aunt, gave me a subscription to the children's *National Geographic* magazine. It was a condensed version of the grown-up mag, the only difference being I had no chance of seeing photographs of topless native women. At the time, I didn't fully understand why this omission didn't bother me. Nor did I understand why cavemen became more intriguing when I read that Neanderthals had builds like modern weight lifters. (This supports my theory that Neanderthals became extinct because homo Homo sapiens looked better to Neanderthal guys than their brow-ridged girlfriends. And homo Homo sapiens liked dating guys who looked like bodybuilders thirty-five thousand years before the Greeks invented gymnasiums.)

The kids' mag heavily promoted the *National Geographic* television specials, and when I read one was going to be about those big-biceped cavemen, I made a point of watching it. "Dr. Leakey and the Dawn of Man" aired in 1966, when I was eight years old. That night my father came home and wanted to watch a football game on television. As he went to change the channel, my mother said, "Tom, Bob wants to watch a *National Geographic Special*." He backed away from the television with "Oh, I didn't know."

I rarely requested to watch any specific program. Christopher Isherwood wrote, "I am a camera with its shutter open, quite passive, recording, not thinking." He offered that as the raison d'être of a writer living in prewar Berlin, but it was also an accurate description of my childhood sitting in front of the television. My viewing was almost godlike; I watched everything. But judging from my impassive response, like God, it was hard to tell if I was enjoying the show.

Most of the time I didn't care about what I watched because watching something boring was almost always better than just being bored. But I wasn't bored by the special about Louis Leakey and his wife, Mary.

To an eight-year-old boy, the Leakeys had the perfect life. They lived in Kenya, but where they worked was in the Olduvai Gorge, a remote area in Tanzania. It was a boy's paradise where lions, giraffes, and other wild animals were common and where the Leakeys slept in tents, which made it seem like they were always on summer vacation. It looked to me that being a paleontologist was a great job. They got paid to play in the dirt and enjoyed the Halloween thrill of digging up skeletons. Somehow I didn't hear the narrator mention that the Leakeys had spent twenty years searching before they discovered their first major find.

In 1966, the two most important discoveries that Louis Leakey had made were actually made by his wife, Mary. In 1948, she discovered a sixteen-million-year-old Miocene primate skull, and then in 1957, while walking her dalmatians, she discovered the almost complete skull of an early australopithecine hominid, which they named Zinjanthropus—a discovery that brought them worldwide fame and led to the financing of their work by the National Geographic Society. (The only disappointment about the special was learning that Zinjanthropus definitely wasn't my type. Too much chimpanzee, not enough Tarzan.)

It never occurred to me while watching Mary Leakey on television that someday I would meet her. When I was a boy, it was easier to imagine meeting dinosaurs and cavemen than it was to imagine meeting people who appeared on television.

In May 1991, at the age of thirty-three, I had decided to go on leave for the summer from my job as a waiter at the Metropolitan Museum of

Art. I was going to perform stand-up comedy in Provincetown, Massa-
chusetts, for six nights a week with my friends Danny McWilliams and
Jaffe Cohen in our show, Funny Gay Males. We had a successful three-
year run at the Duplex in New York, but this was a pivotal step. We were
all quitting our day jobs and going to try to earn our living primarily
with our comedy. I was beset by doubts that I would ever make a living
as an out gay comedian. But I also thought of all my friends who had
died of AIDS. If I was lucky enough to be alive, it seemed wrong not to
try to do what I wanted to do with my life.

On May 15, a month before we would leave for Provincetown, I was
hired to work as a cater waiter at the commencement dinner thrown by
the president of Columbia University. The man in charge of the party
was named Victor, and he looked normal enough until you noticed the
teensy five-inch braided ponytail dangling down the back of his neck. It
made me wonder if he was still angry and had never forgiven his father
for not letting him play with dolls and this embarrassingly unattractive
hairstyle was his revenge. At the start of every job, Victor liked to let
people know he was in charge, but he did this with such wistfulness that
every command seemed like a vague yearning rather than an order.

I had overheard Victor mention one of the guests of honor at the
dinner, and I asked him, "Did you say that Mary Leakey is getting an
honorary degree?"

"Yeah, who is she?"

"Who's Mary Leakey?"

I felt like the sole remaining devoted fan of a forgotten silent movie
star.

"She's Mary Leakey . . . of the Leakeys."

Victor's expression didn't change, and I realized that not everyone
had watched every *National Geographic Special* while growing up. (I
hadn't thought about Mary Leakey in years, but my excitement after
hearing her name made me feel eight again.) After Louis's death in 1972,
Mary became a public figure in her own right. She went on to lead an

expedition to excavate a site at Laetoli, Tanzania, that had interested her for decades. It was at this site in 1976 that a member of Mary's team made a major find. In the volcanic ash that covered the Laetoli site was a trail of perfectly preserved 3.5-million-year-old hominid footprints that proved conclusively that walking upright happened much earlier than suspected. (Unless measured by the scale of a lifetime, 3.5 million years is an unimaginable span of time. Using thirty years as a generation, the footprints in Laetoli could have been made by my great-great—plus 117,000 more greats—grandparents.)

At first glance the trail of footsteps suggested only two hominids, but a careful examination led to the discovery that inside the larger footsteps were another set of smaller footprints almost as if a child was playing follow the leader. To me it seemed incredible that less than ten years after man had first walked on the moon, evidence of the first steps of man on earth were discovered.

When Mary Leakey entered the president's house, I recognized her immediately. She had the dowdy, I-can't-be-bothered-about-my-appearance look of a distracted intellectual who's smart enough to know the speed of light but too dumb to use sunblock. After sixty years of working outdoors, Mary Leakey's face had developed several prominent moles that were arranged in a kind of disorganized Stonehenge.

Mrs. Leakey was one of the guests of honor, but I noticed during the dinner there were long periods where she was ignored even by the people seated next to her. At first this shocked—and then infuriated—me. She was seventy-eight, and I couldn't believe that people weren't curious about her life and work. She wasn't a second-rate celebrity. Mary Leakey had made discoveries that were scientifically important and also poetically evocative of what it means to be human. I was thrilled to be in the same room with her and decided all the other guests were idiots. When Mary looked bored, I hated them. I went over to Tom, my boyfriend at the time, to point her out and let off steam about the academic drudges who weren't showing any interest in her. My conversation with him was dissatisfying because he sympathized with the drudges since he wasn't interested in her either. He gave me his polite attention before mocking me with "Bob, it's not like she's Barbra Streisand."

During the dinner, Victor asked me with his usual deference if I would later serve after-dinner drinks in the library. ("Bob, would you mind, but only if you don't mind, if you do, let me know, I'll try to find someone else, could you . . . maybe, um . . . would you set up the bar in the library for the after-dinner drinks? If that's okay?") I agreed and went into the library after coffee was served. As soon as the dinner ended, most of the guests began to leave. I was glad of this and assumed I wasn't going to be too busy.

To my surprise, Mary Leakey wandered in by herself. I couldn't believe it. Like any devoted fan, I had read her autobiography, *Disclosing the Past*, and knew that she was fond of a glass of single malt and even a good cigar at the end of the day. So I immediately asked her, "Mrs. Leakey, can I get you something to drink?"

She smiled when I recognized her. "I'd love a Jack Daniels on the rocks."

Cater waiters are not supposed to converse with the guests, but I understood this would be my only opportunity to talk to her. I easily stepped over the velvet rope that separates the public from a star. As I poured her drink, I said, "Mrs. Leakey, I'm a big fan of yours." When the words came out of my mouth, I realized how absurd I sounded, but real fans are unstoppable. I pushed on with "When I was a boy, I saw the *National Geographic Special* about your work, and I've always wondered what it was like to discover the footprints at Lee . . . ."

I was so excited that the name of the footprint site slipped my mind. She'll think I'm an idiot, I thought. But she smiled and helped me out, "Laetoli."

When I handed her her drink, she added, "That was possibly the most significant discovery that I played a part in. The excitement was quite intense when we realized what we had found."

Under my incessant questioning, she talked briefly about some of her other experiences: tracing cave paintings in Tanzania, finding a huge deposit of Stone Age axes, the discovery of the Zinjanthropus skull. It was at this point that she looked directly at me and said, "I've always been curious. That's what kept me searching." She then took a sip of her drink and asked me about myself.

"I'm a stand-up comic," I said.

She stared at me at me as if a tibia was sticking out of my head.

"You're funny?"

Her skeptical tone seemed to say I'd need hard evidence to prove my theory.

"Yes," I answered, thinking I'm not about to tell Mary Leakey a joke and risk bombing. I mentioned I was nervous about quitting my day job to go away to perform for three months.

"Oh, you can't let that be an obstacle," she said. "I've always done exactly what I wanted and I've had a wonderful life."

Mary spoke with a sense of pride and a trace of maternal asperity. It was startling, as I'd never heard anyone claim to have lived a wonderful life before. At that moment it became absolutely clear to me that leading a curious life is the most practical thing a person can do. Suddenly I understood that I had made Mary's evening—and she had made mine. It's a rare event when a conversation turns into an epiphany, almost as infrequent as finding an Australopithecus skull while out walking your dogs. At that moment it became absolutely clear that I would be happy spending my life searching for farcical, hysterical, and witty.

Coffee Point

Travel guides should advise their readers that the easiest way to fall in love with a place is to have hot sex there. I discovered this for myself since hooking up in Alaska just made me more smitten with our forty-ninth state. Until I visited Alaska, I had never thought of myself as adventurous—ignoring that I'd been performing stand-up comedy since I turned eighteen and several years later moved to New York City without a clear ambition other than to get out of Buffalo.

When *Out* magazine hired me to write an article, my editor asked me to suggest a subject. I immediately said that I wanted to write about gay people in Alaska. The previous year, I'd performed stand-up comedy in Anchorage at a benefit for Alaska's gay rights organization, Identity, and met an extraordinary group of men and women.

A lesbian and her partner let me stay with them in their sprawling ranch house to conserve the group's funds. (I've often done this to save money for LGBT groups, and my approval rating is 100 percent. The gays would never let your host or hosts be less than fabulous.) Marge was an expert musician in playing accordions, concertinas, and squeeze-boxes of all sorts. She had an all-women band called Marge and the Polka Chips that performed all over Alaska. Often, they were hired to celebrate the end of crabbing season and would be flown out to Dutch Harbor in the Aleutians.

At my performance in Anchorage at the Fourth Avenue Theater—a streamline moderne landmark movie palace built in the forties that survived Alaska's catastrophic 1964 earthquake—I was seated at a table that changed my path for my life. I met two partnered doctors who were instrumental in setting up the Native Health Service, where community health practitioners were trained for eight weeks, then given a handbook detailing treatment for every sort of medical emergency plus a radio that could be used to call for help. Thus prepared, the health practitioners were sent to serve in remote Native villages. The two docs assured me that their system worked and later investigating their claims, I discovered that it did. Seated on my right was Vic Carlson, a retired judge who was a fierce advocate for LGBT rights, and to my left was Brad Williams, a handsome thirty-two-year-old, copper-haired, blue-eyed salmon fisherman.

After the benefit, Brad asked me if I wanted to go out for a drink at Mad Myrna's, Anchorage's principal gay bar. He had a new pickup truck, which was not the usual vehicle for gay guys in Los Angeles, where I lived at the time. This pleased me since it reminded me of my close friend Michael Hart, who lived in Santa Fe and also drove a pickup. It sounds as if I was impressed with the butchness of driving a truck. That was part of it, but to me it was a sign that I might have found another adventurous friend.

Brad met my requirements for being a close friend. He was a gay man who would rather go camping on a prairie than see a production of *Oklahoma!* (Admittedly, I do have plenty of friends who prefer listening to *The Sound of Music*'s "Climb Ev'ry Mountain" rather than hiking up any peak.)

On that first visit to Alaska, we made the drive from Anchorage down to Seward in two and a half hours. No tourist ever makes the trip in that amount of time since it's one of the most scenic drives in the world and at some point a panorama will compel you to pull over. There's a vitality to the landscape that makes everything seem fresh: clouds, sky, mountains, creeks, rivers, oceans—even trees. I've subsequently made the trip several times, and the comedian in me always insists on stopping at the Tesoro gas station and convenience store at the turn-off to Girdwood, Anchorage's ski resort.

The convenience store faces Turnagain Arm, an inlet named by William Bligh—the *Mutiny on the Bounty* captain. He was then the sailing master on Captain Cook's third and final voyage. Towering over the inlet are majestic snowcapped mountains. It's the meeting point between America the beautiful and America the ugly and sarcastically emphasizes that every American is a citizen of both countries. If you're going to litter the landscape with a jumbo Slurpee cup, you couldn't pick a better spot.

It was the first week of October and the aspens and birches had turned, but their yellow leaves were shivering as if winter was an hour away. I've been to Alaska sixteen times, and it always evokes a complementary mix of exhilaration and pride. Part of me is always thinking, "Wow! I'm in Alaska!" while simultaneously congratulating myself, "Wow! I'm happy!"

In Seward, we went on a cruise to see Kenai Fjords National Park and on our way ran into a super pod of killer whales. In the fall, orcas form large groups, and surrounding our ship were fifty whales. Standing on the deck of the boat, in the omnipresent Alaskan drizzle, I watched four dorsal fins rising like claws from the sea all around us while everywhere else I looked a whale was breaching. Another passenger on the ship exclaimed, "This is spectacular! And I'm from Montana." His amusing endorsement reminded me that Alaska had always intrigued me.

Part of my love of Alaska will always be linked to my vitriolic disgust and hatred for antienvironmental fanatics. All through the seventies, I followed the Alaska Native Claims Settlement of 1971, the failed attempts to create new national parks in Alaska in 1974, and Jimmy Carter proclaiming all the designated Alaska parklands as national monuments in

1978 under the National Antiquities Act. When I was twenty-two in 1980, I was relieved and thrilled when President Carter signed the Alaska National Interest Lands Conservation Act, which doubled the size of our national park system, shortly before the antienvironmental Reagan took office.

People forget there was a time when protecting the environment was nonpartisan. Republican president Teddy Roosevelt created our national forests, Eisenhower created the Arctic National Wildlife Refuge, and Nixon created the Environmental Protection Agency and signed the Endangered Species Act. But Ronnie thought being green meant making money by sucking on the planet like a leech. He enjoyed the outdoors at his private ranch in California while he tried to trash our public lands with logging, mining, and oil and gas drilling. He was the first of the selfish right-wing fucks who have their ranches or oceanfront houses but don't give a damn about our national parks, forests, and wildlife refuges. It's as if these loathsome morons think sharing the planet with other life forms is communism.

Reagan's appointment of James Watt, a fundamentalist Christian antienvironmentalist, as our secretary of the interior infuriated me. Watt seemed to want to cut down all our forests so there was no chance Jesus would be crucified after his second coming. In response, I joined the Nature Conservancy and the Wilderness Society and even donated extra money to both organizations when I was barely earning enough to pay my New York City rent.

When I contacted Brad about my article for *Out* magazine, he told me that I couldn't just interview gay men and lesbians living in Anchorage. I needed to get out in the bush. Brad invited me to come salmon fishing with him at Coffee Point on Bristol Bay, out on the Alaska peninsula. I said, "Yes," since my previous trip had convinced me that when an Alaskan invites you to do something outdoors the smart answer is always "Yes!"

On the summer solstice, I returned to Anchorage and stayed with Vic Carlson, the retired judge, and his partner, Jerry. Vic is a tall, handsome, elderly man with a neatly trimmed white beard, but his most distinguishing feature is his deep, authoritative voice. It's the perfect voice for a judge since he sounds like Jehovah in a Cecil B. DeMille film. Vic and Jerry live in downtown Anchorage in a historic neighborhood near Delaney Park, where the architecture varies from log cabins to houses from the thirties that look like astronomical observatories to hideous suburban monstrosities built in the seventies during the pipeline boom.

I soon learned that Vic seemed to know every gay man and lesbian in Alaska. If I mentioned his name in Juneau or Fairbanks, there was always someone in the group who was a friend of Vic's. He always threw dinner parties when I visited—serving excellent fresh salmon or halibut—and his guests ranged from Native Alaskan college students to lovely lesbians who worked at the art museum to the most rugged muscular interior decorator the world has ever known. One of Vic's friends, a silver-daddy Paul Bunyan, told me, "I love opera and love my chain saw." Through his friends, Vic was instrumental in making me see that gay people in Alaska should be celebrated.

Vic explained that he first visited Alaska when he was in the army and stationed in the Aleutians. In 1963, when he was in his late twenties, he moved to Fairbanks. It's a story I've heard many times, and I'm convinced that if I had visited Alaska in my twenties, I too would have headed north.

I posted a notice about the purpose of my visit in a chat room for gay Alaskans and heard from dozens of LGBT Alaskans. One of the people who contacted me was Jim Wilkins, a handsome Inupiat Native Alaskan. We had dinner at a restaurant—in Alaska, always order salmon or halibut—and then he showed me the remarkable downtown fishing in Anchorage on Ship Creek where huge three-foot-long king salmon were caught by the locals. Then we went back to my room at Vic's to make out.

The next day, I flew on a commercial jet to the airport at the village of King Salmon, the regional hub for the Alaska peninsula. At breakfast, Vic had grinned and told me, "You're going to do something most Alaskans never experience."

His comment excited me since I've always sought out the path less traveled. (Although getting a rare life-threatening disease versus coming down with a common cold makes me think I need to ease up on my predilection for idiosyncrasy.) Vic had advised me to bring fresh food as a thank you gift since at Coffee Point a trip to the nearest supermarket required an airplane. I bought some expensive frozen steaks, some fancy bakery bread, and salad fixings. On my flight to King Salmon, we flew over snow-covered mountains that looked close enough to crash into. After landing, I hired a bush pilot for two hundred dollars to fly me forty miles, to Egegik—pronounced Iggy-gick—the Native village across the river from where Brad fished. Egegik was 326 miles southwest of Anchorage, almost exactly the same distance between Portland, Maine, and New York City. Alaska is big.

We then took off from Egegik and looped over Coffee Point, giving me a clear view of all the fishing boats in the bay, the abandoned cannery along the Egegik River, and the collection of shacks and airplane hangars that comprised the summer fishing camp. The pilot left me standing on the gravel runway, carrying two heavy duffel bags.

The wind was snapping a signal flag on a pole, and I saw the top of a snow-streaked mountain to the southeast. Brad would later tell me it was Mount Peulik, an active volcano. A shack stood nearby, and behind me were miles of scrubby bushes, interspersed with tundra and ponds. It felt as if I had stepped through the looking glass of a frontier saloon. Moving toward the shack, my hiking boots puddled in the dry grass that camouflaged swampy mud. With every step, I teeter-tottered until I reached the shack. A middle-aged woman whose gray hair looked like an impenetrable old-growth forest—also the norm in Alaska—was fixing her four-wheel ATV. I was relieved that she knew Brad Williams and could direct me down toward the shore through a street of haphazardly placed shacks, which looked as if they'd been assembled from flotsam that had washed up on the beach. Every yard was littered with oil drums, fishing nets, an ATV, and a rusting, wind-battered pickup truck that mirrored Coffee Point's architecture. The housing wasn't pretty, but it got the job done during sockeye season in June and July.

I found Brad in his yard, dressed in waders, stacking plastic totes that were either labeled with Magic Marker "water" or "ice" or held fish. His welcoming smile had an element of astonishment. Later, Brad admitted he'd had severe doubts that I would make the trip. I was the first friend of his to ever visit Coffee Point—and he had been a commercial fisherman since he was eight years old.

Brad's house was on the bluff looking out on Bristol Bay, although the beach view was blocked by the sauna house, which had been built by Brad's older brother, Dave. The sauna house had a picture window that allowed you to steam while giving you a spectacular view of the midnight sun setting over the ocean—horizoned with fishing boats. ("Spectacular" is the most overused adjective in Alaska, equivalent to the overused "fabulous" by the gays.)

We went inside the small house and entered the kitchen. There was an oak table with three mismatched chairs, a bathroom, and a tiny bedroom with a mattress on the floor. I especially liked the turquoise enamel gas stove that looked vintage 1960s. There were gray carpeted steps leading to the second floor. After removing our boots, we climbed the stairs and entered a spotless all-white room with three picture windows that offered a breathtaking panoramic view of Coffee Point. The fourth wall was a bed alcove with a handy thick blue curtain that blocked the sunrise at 3:00 a.m.

Looking out over the water, it struck me that this was better than tourist Alaska—and tourist Alaska is great; I was actually going to live like an Alaskan. Brad took me for a ride on his four-wheeler to show me around Coffee Point. Initially, I felt awkward about wrapping my arms around his waist but got over it quickly, as it was the only way I could hang on. We zoomed down to the Egegik River and saw a shack with a No Trespassing sign. Brad explained the owner was a kook who would pull a gun on you if you stepped on his property. We both mocked the idea of thinking anyone needed to fear strangers at Coffee Point.

We stopped at a pond where I looked down and saw three-inch-high irises and chocolate lilies at our feet. They had adapted to the ceaseless icy wind coming off the bay by hunkering down. When I pointed them out to Brad, he said, "I've never noticed them before."

"You don't notice beautiful wildflowers?"

"Hot pansies always get my attention."

Later, we got in Brad's truck to check his setnet, which was three miles down the beach. His truck reeked of salmon; I jokingly said the stink was like salmon ass. When I went to roll down the window, Brad warned me, "The mosquitoes are worse than the smell." I rolled it back up. "You'll get used to it," he said and I soon did.

There were two ways to catch sockeye salmon at Coffee Point: either from a boat or from a setnet on shore. Brad's brother was out crewing on a boat, and every inch of beach was lined with setnets. The nets hung perpendicular to the shore, positioned to catch salmon swimming toward the Egegik River. Brad went out in a rubber raft and picked the fish from his net and threw them in his raft. He surrounded himself with two-foot salmon, getting coated with their slime and blood, which explained his truck's aroma. Other people picked salmon from aluminum boats, but Brad took pride in fishing as cheaply as he could, often buying his equipment at garage sales in Anchorage or in his hometown of Homer.

Brad knew I liked bird-watching and insisted on stopping at an airplane hangar to show me a nest of ravens. The baby ravens looked cartoonishly evil, like characters in an Edward Gorey drawing. As we drove down the beach, Brad stopped to show me a falcon that had built a nest in an abandoned construction crane on the beach, the tallest point for forty miles. I raised my binoculars and saw that it was too pale to be a peregrine. Looking it up later in a bird guide, I decided it was a merlin.

The new birds that fascinated me were long-tailed jaegers, which are about the size of large seagulls, except they have a beautiful, long, streamlined art deco tail. The jaegers often hovered over the same spot, gliding in the constant wind along the beach, patiently waiting for a dead salmon to wash up on shore. The beach was wide and ended at a twenty-five-foot bluff. It was used as a highway by the setnetters. As Brad drove, he waved to every passing driver. There were only a few hundred fishermen at Coffee Point, and after a few summers you knew everyone by sight. We saw struggling salmon in Brad's net as he parked his truck. Lacking a crew permit, I couldn't legally help Brad, which was fine with me, since I was supposedly working as a reporter.

On the bluff above every site, there was a sign with the setnet permit number of each fisherman. All the signs were white except for Brad's, which was lime green. When I commented on his color choice, he laughed and said, "I thought I'd gay it up."

There was a notch where the bluff had collapsed, and I climbed up and sat near the edge while Brad paddled out along his net. My seat was dry as the bluff was sand, and rain quickly drained away. The tundra was a mix of plants, little evergreens, tiny white flowers, and miniature marvels in every shade of green and red. I stared in fascination at the most beautiful lawn on earth. A bald eagle landed twenty feet away from me, surveying the beach for a salmon dinner. Brad said there were brown bears at Coffee Point, but I never saw one. I walked inland for a short distance and spooked my first ptarmigan. The ptarmigan is Alaska's grouse, and it scooted along the ground like it was embarrassed to be seen, being half-dressed with brown summer feathers interspersed with white winter plumage. The next day—poking around the shore while

Brad picked sockeyes—I discovered a dead male spectacled eider, nestled in a clump of beach grass. A threatened species, it's a beautiful sea duck with a pale green head and eyes that are surrounded by white feathers and black spectacles. I thought they only lived farther north and west in the Yukon Delta. It must have just died since it had showed no signs of decay. I felt sad and elated, which I didn't realize then is the default setting for most of our emotional lives.

After picking salmon, Brad had to empty his raft by throwing the fish into white plastic totes on the back of his truck. Then we drove his catch down to the cannery weigh station back at Coffee Point. That summer, it was run by three young guys from Boulder, Colorado, who sought out adventurous summer jobs in Alaska. They lived in a Quonset hut on-site and were jokingly friendly with Brad since he let them use his sauna. A visitor at Coffee Point was as rare as seventy-degree summer weather, and they welcomed me with genuine warmth and pride in their rugged life. Soon I was cracking jokes with them about Brad's stinky truck.

The first thing one of the guys did when we pulled up was shovel chopped ice over Brad's fish. Then another guy removed each tote from the back of the truck with a forklift, letting fountains of blood gush over the sand from four holes in the bottom of the container. For an instant, the tote looked like a dinner table for Dracula. Brad's catch was then weighed and tallied. The cannery paid every fisherman at the end of the season.

At the end of the day, we always took a sauna. No bathing in the morning, which surprisingly was kind of liberating. Since everyone was grubby at Coffee Point, we were all equally skanky. In the sauna house, there was an oil drum filled with clean warm water next to a rock pile heated by a wood-burning stove. We gathered our sauna wood from the beach and showered with a coffee-can ladle, but this still felt like the most luxurious bath on earth. Afterward, we sat our clean bodies on a built-in bench and looked out the window on the setting midnight sun and felt like the luckiest guys alive.

On my second night, I took a can of beer into the sauna even though Brad had warned me that drinking in the sauna can make you pass out. I'm not sure why I ignored his advice, but I'm glad I did. We got up to leave and I fainted. I came to with Brad holding me up outside the sauna, our faces inches from each other.

The same thought occurred to both of us, and we began kissing. We were both naked and broke off our long, passionate face-sucking when the mosquitoes biting our asses trumped the pleasure our lips and tongues were receiving. After we finished our smooch, Brad commented, "It's about time!"

We both acknowledged that we thought the other wasn't interested. Evolution really should have evolved a pheromone that works like a fart: letting the room know you're horny. Or even a phero-moan, a grunt that signals you're in the mood. Brad insisted on latching on to me as we walked to the house, and I was more than happy to be steadied by a handsome muscular guy. Then we did what two stirred-up animals do— we had sex.

The next morning was rainy, and Brad listened to his radio before heading out to pick salmon. Every day, he had to listen to an announcement from the Alaska Department of Fish and Game to learn whether fishing was closed. The department monitored the sockeyes returning to the Egegik River and sporadically closed fishing in order to keep the Bristol Bay fishery sustainable. This is the largest, most ecologically intact salmon fishery in the world. The fishermen supported being regulated since they wanted to preserve their livelihoods, and pauses in the fishing also gave everyone a needed break.

Brad headed out while I kept drinking coffee and writing at the kitchen table in my black-and-white notebook. I ended up writing sixty pages of notes since I wasn't sure what I would use in my magazine piece. After an hour, I decided to walk down the beach to meet Brad. My personal "Call of the Wild" is whatever makes my heart thump, and the Alaskan outdoors during the summer and a hunky fisherman were howling for me.

I had barely started down the beach before a battered pickup stopped and a tough elderly woman rolled down the window and barked, "Get in!" She was Brad's setnet neighbor, Mary Wickersham. She was teaching her granddaughter how to fish. Gruff is an inadequate word to describe Mary. She probably could have shouted, "Get in!" on the beach and hundreds of salmon would have headed into her net. Mary chain-smoked all the time but didn't believe cigarettes caused her early symptoms of emphysema. During the ride, she asked, "Who do you know in Alaska?" I jokingly said, "I know Marge of Marge and the Polka Chips."

"I know Marge!" she shouted. "I've heard her on the radio!"

This was funny, but it also made me feel Alaska was a magical place: not just due to the scenery and wildlife—but due to Alaskans themselves. I had found my middle-earth where connections were being made, but I didn't understand where I was journeying. When we got to Brad's site, he asked Mary if she would help him untangle his net. For the next hour, she repeatedly drove her truck into the surf and up and down the beach until the problem was solved.

On the drive to the weigh station, I expressed my admiration for Mary's thoughtfulness. Brad explained that people would always help you at Coffee Point. Of course, there was the kook with the no trespassing sign. But even he would lend a hand if you asked—as long as you didn't step on his property. Houses were left unlocked; if you needed something from a neighbor, you could run in and borrow it. Brad always left his truck keys in the ignition since no one was going to steal a vehicle that couldn't be driven farther than five miles.

It dawned on me why I loved Coffee Point. It looked like a shanty-town, but the setting was beautiful and so were its uncombed, mildly stinky inhabitants. Coffee Point was a two-month utopia every year.

That day, the guys at the weigh station gave me a huge king salmon. Sockeyes were the normal catch, but kings were occasionally caught and usually eaten by the Coffee Point fisherman. Brad's neighbor and friend was a woman fisherman named Stacey Clark. She was a tall, slim, attractive, long-haired, dangly-earring-wearing, cool fishing chick in her late thirties—with a hot, new semislacker boyfriend every summer. She offered to clean my salmon either for shipping in dry ice back to Los Angeles or for eating that night. Brad told me this was a major gift. During the rest of the year, Stacey cleaned salmon for a company that sold smoked salmon, and she was renowned for her expert deboning.

We decided to organize a feast for that evening. The celebration was held at Stacey's house, which had a large bright red kitchen. Above her sink was a window overlooking the bay. Somehow the image of washing dishes while enjoying a million-dollar view became emblematic of Coffee Point and of my vision of how to live. Work hard but enjoy your life.

We invited Mary and her granddaughter. Brad and Stacey's studly boyfriend grilled my steaks, and we had three kinds of salmon. One was pickled salmon made by the chain-smoking Mary. It appeared to be medical specimens floating in a jar but startled me with its savory deliciousness. We also had sockeye salmon fried with wild mushrooms picked by Stacey in the forests of Homer. That was my scrumptious favorite of our trio. In addition to those, there was my grilled king salmon. I had worked as a cater waiter for years in New York, but that meal was one of the best I've ever eaten. The steak, salad, baked potatoes, and homemade chocolate chip cookies for dessert all seemed as new to my tongue as the landscape was to my eyes.

While the guys grilled our steaks and salmon, we also drank plenty of red wine and smoked pot. This was my introduction to smoking marijuana in Alaska, which I would learn was a recreational activity that Alaskans enjoy even more than fishing and hunting. In Alaska, bear attacks are just considered a bad case of the munchies.

The next day was my last full day at Coffee Point, and fishing was closed for twelve hours. Brad made pancakes for breakfast with bits of dark chocolate sprinkled in them. Then we drove down the beach to pull in his net. It was sunny with clear skies. We climbed to the top of the bluff, where it was so warm we took off our jackets and sat down.

Brad spotted two bald eagles sitting on a ridge, and then he told me that when he was a boy he liked walking barefoot on the tundra. "Take off your boots and socks," he ordered.

I did what he asked. Brad's advice had brought me to Coffee Point, and by then I trusted him completely about what I should do in Alaska. He also removed his boots and socks. We walked barefoot across the tundra, which was delightfully spongy—but not wet or cold. There were no sharp sticks or rocks, and each step was blissful. The experience was comic and cosmic, which is the best life has to offer. I imagined Brad as a little boy discovering this and knew the past four days had been extraordinary.

That afternoon, we went to get water for the sauna at a natural spring down on the Egegik River. The water slowly dripped out of the bluff, and it took about an hour to fill two totes. While waiting, we lay in a bower of dry brown grasses that was embroidered with the green shoots of one-inch-wide wild lavender geraniums. It was sunny, and our grass- and flower-lined nest shielded us from the wind. We felt warm and stripped off our shirts and sunbathed. (We got sunburned, and you haven't lived until you've fried on the tundra.)

Brad and I digressed about our families, failed romances, and dreams. He was studying journalism at the University of Alaska while also learning Japanese, since he had an office job at the Japanese consulate in Anchorage. I had a second collection of comic essays coming out that fall but was uncertain what to write next.

The next morning was my departure, and after breakfast we went upstairs to enjoy the view and were just about to have sex when we heard my plane fly overhead. We laughed at our interruptus and packed up our packages. Brad and I kissed good-bye in his house, hopped on his four-wheeler, and raced to the plane. (There was a road to the runway strip that I hadn't noticed when I arrived.) The pilot was standing next to his plane, and we hurriedly stowed my much-lighter luggage. A quick hug and I was soon in the air.

At the airport at King Salmon, I had an hour wait for my flight to Anchorage. There was a tiny gift shop, and I was startled by another example of Alaskan serendipity. There was a copy for sale of the memoir *This Is Coffee Point, Go Ahead: A Mother's Story of Fishing & Survival at Alaska's Bristol Bay*, written by Brad's mom, Wilma Williams. I bought it, a *Newsweek*, and a copy of the regional paper, the *Bristol Bay Times*.

In *Newsweek*, I read a short notice about how Mark Wahlberg had prepared for his role as a fisherman in the film *The Perfect Storm* by going fishing for a month. I immediately imagined a hunky actor getting into character by coming to Coffee Point with Brad and me. Then I read an article in the *Bristol Bay Times* about how Alaska had the highest rate of botulism in the country.

This was due to Native communities using Tupperware to store traditional foods, such as stinkheads, which are fermented salmon heads that traditionally had been safely stored in grass-lined pits. The two stories clanged in my imagination as I pictured an actor getting botulism due to his playing a Native Alaskan fisherman. I admired the comic novels of Evelyn Waugh, who used his travels as the basis for many of his books. Perhaps I could write a comic novel about Alaska.

On the flight back to Los Angeles, I felt dreamily romantic and thought I'd fallen in love with Brad, when it turned out I'd fallen in love with Alaska.

Nature Boys

My four best friends and I identify as gay, but we're probably bisexual since we've each had a longer relationship with Mother Nature than with any guy. My closest pals are Michael Hart, Eddie Sarfaty, John Arnold, and my partner, Michael Zam. (I have close women friends too, but they can't even agree on how to spell womyn.)

Claiming to have four best friends sounds like I'm bragging. It's true though: they are my best friends, and they also share my love of nature. They're Nature Boys. They love to hike and canoe and they love animals. John and Eddie have adopted rescued cats, and the two Michaels have adopted rescued dogs. They'd adopt rescued whales and eagles if they could.

The adjective "rescued" is important as it's also an indicator of a moral quality they all share. These guys would never litter a forest, drill for petroleum in the Arctic National Wildlife Refuge, or not help a blind woman cross a street. They're irreverent and kind, and they all have great senses of humor. Being friends with someone unfunny is like having a lover who doesn't enjoy sex. What's the point?

John is an architect, Michael Hart is in the furniture business—both building and selling—Eddie is a fellow stand-up comic and writer, and Michael Zam is a writer of screenplays and plays and my reason for living. Of course, they're all handsome. (It could be that I'm shallow, but I prefer to think of it as liking scenery.)

Fortunately, our friendship hasn't changed since I had to be the first of my buddies to get a you're-gonna-die-agnosis. I have ALS. (That abbreviation stands for Asinine Life-threatening Sickness, according to me.)

My Nature Boys have been flippant and humane about my predicament. Navigating a treacherous disease requires the same skills as a hiker. With a life-threatening illness, you have to treat the Angel of Death like he's a skunk. Avoid getting too close, or you'll be stinking like a rotting corpse. Your life has changed direction, and you could easily get lost dealing only with your health, which would be like strolling through a redwood forest dwelling on filing your taxes. You need to be present in your life—not contemplating your afterlife.

It took a life-threatening illness to make me see that the reason most of us love the natural world is because it's a visual and vocal echo that we're alive. Every mosquito bite is a painful pat on the back that we're still fresh enough to be lunch. We focus on the green in a forest, while gently ignoring that every fallen leaf is a brown Post-it note from Mother Nature that someday we'll all be dead.

Years before my first symptoms, I was climbing Mount Cardigan in New Hampshire with John and Eddie, and we moved steadily upward until I reached a spot where I couldn't figure out my next hand and foothold. I looked down for the first time on our hike and was astonished to see I was hanging on a cliff with a hundred-foot drop.

"I'm stuck."

John and Eddie were higher up the mountain.

"Bob," said John. "We don't hike with slackers."

"I'm a wallflower."

There was no way to backtrack and, for a moment, I imagined plummeting to my death. My heavy Leica binoculars were swinging unsteadily, hitting the cliff, my neck, and even my face. John worried they were hindering me. He descended a few feet, but I was too far down the mountain. I insisted that the binoculars weren't a problem, thinking that I didn't want John to plunge to his death helping me. Eddie jokingly asked if he should use his cell to call for a rescue helicopter. "Could you request their hunkiest rescue team?" I replied. It took about half an hour, but with John and Eddie's encouragement—and derisive comments—I was able to clamber up the mountain instead of ascending to heaven.

My Nature Boys aren't peacenik hippies putting flowers in gun barrels. They're more likely to hand a daisy to a greedy CEO and tell him to shove it up his ass. I'd like to tell God what a dick he is for creating ALS and punch him—if I could still make a fist. He might send me to hell for my disrespect, but I know my Nature Boys would back me up. It's heartening to feel that in their afterlives, your best friends would pester God for billions of years: "Where's Bob?"

Since I've lost the ability to speak, it pains me that my limited communication—everything's typed out on my iPad—might harm my bond with my closest friends. When I first met John, Eddie, Michael, and Michael, there was an immediate connection with each of them— usually a one-liner—and over the years those cords of humor have been woven into cables of love.

There are also times when jokes don't work as lifelines. My Nature Boys and I have been through the inevitable pain and wounds that all living things have to endure. Instead of a tick making life miserable for a deer, we've seen friends die of AIDS, sibling suicides, bad relationships, mean breakups, deaths of parents, and the caterpillar of depression munching on our thoughts.

Recently, in Provincetown, Eddie and I saw our first pod of right whales. They're an endangered species. There are only about four hundred in the North Atlantic since they were the "right" whales to kill. We stood on the sand dunes at Race Point watching a half dozen of them playfully breaching off shore. It made me happy, but it was also odd. Whales are big-brained mammals that can't communicate with us. My illness has destroyed my voice and made me feel increasingly like an intelligent animal who's trapped in his head. Because I have to type out every thought, half of my observations remain brainwaves. Even writing about my illness makes me feel I'm bellyaching—and I loathe perpetual gripers. But, right now, not writing about my ALS wouldn't be telling my entire story.

I saw my first rattlesnake with John. We were hiking with his father in the Malibu hills. It was early in the year—one of the first hot days—and as we walked the trail, I recalled that rattlesnakes often warmed up their cold blood after the winter. I'd never seen a rattlesnake and had wanted to see one since I was a little boy. Being especially observant that day, I noticed a rustling in the tall grasses by the side of the trail. Sticking my head over the stalks, I spotted a brown three-foot-long Southern Pacific rattlesnake as thick as a himbo's wrist. The snake had stopped moving, and I called to John and his dad. As soon as the three of us started staring, the snake twisted into a coil and gave his rattle a shake. He seemed rightfully annoyed, as we were the ones threatening him. John and I kept a reasonable distance since that species carries highly toxic venom, but John's dad was curious and moved within fanging range. It's not right when the kids have to warn the parent to be careful.

Michael Hart and I went on a camping trip to Canyon de Chelly in Arizona and Chaco Canyon in New Mexico. We visited Chaco Canyon, an isolated national park, during the first week of September, when the purple aster bushes, *aster bigelovii*, with their lavender-and-yellow blossoms were flowering. The park had only a handful of other visitors, and the sight of the blooming bushes covering the desolate ruins of the capital of the Anasazi culture was otherworldly. I was healthy and fit then but can see now that it's better not to ponder that every flower on earth sprouts on the grave of some living thing.

At Canyon de Chelly, a Navaho woman was selling petrified wood. She had a tribal permit to sell the pieces, which made Michael and me think it was okay for us to soft sell ourselves and that by buying petrified wood from her, we were helping feed her family—not trafficking in looted fossils. We bought two firewood-sized logs for twenty bucks each. (There was no haggling. I had collected rocks since I was a kid and knew this was a good deal.) At the time, it didn't register that I was buying a living thing that had died and been transformed into its own beautiful red, yellow, and orange tombstone.

Michael lived in Santa Fe and during a Christmas visit, we drove down to the Bosque del Apache National Wildlife Refuge, where you can see fourteen thousand wintering sandhill cranes, thirty-four thousand Ross's and snow geese, and also the bald eagles, prairie falcons, and coyotes stalking the birds. I've visited the refuge several times. It's always like watching a wildlife documentary, although it can be brutal. I'll never forget seeing a bald eagle triumphantly gripping a bloody snow goose on a frozen pond.

I've probably given you a wrong impression because most of my excursions into the outdoors have been more merry than morbid. Eddie and I did a stand-up show together at Russian River in California, where I was able to show him his first redwoods at Armstrong Redwoods State Natural Reserve. The reserve is 805 acres, almost the same size as 843-acre Central Park. Redwoods make you think you've never seen a tree before.

"No wonder you love redwoods," said Eddie as we walked through the grove. "They're California bodybuilder trees."

I laughed. "You're right. They're strapping hunks."

"You same-sex tree hugger."

"I did have sex here."

I told Eddie about the handsome blond I met at one of John Arnold's parties. We dated for six months and one time, when I had a gig at Russian River, I brought him along.

"The park was empty, and he blew me in the notch of an old redwood."

"You're the only guy I know who's had a three-way with a tree."

This might be too much information, but Nature Boys enjoy sex and believe people who think sex is dirty probably imagine French kissing is unhygienic and insist on both partners wearing tongue condoms. Walking through a redwood forest, you wonder why anyone would want to cut them down. I owned a house in Los Angeles that was built in the 1920s and was horrified to learn that it was built out of redwood. It's like building a baby stroller out of baby bones.

My partner, Michael Zam, loves animals, though he's hilariously afraid of mice and can't watch a nature documentary where there's any bloodshed. Our first nature expedition was to Joshua Tree National Park. On our way to the park, we passed the Big Morongo Canyon Preserve, a spot I've visited with each of my Nature Boys. It has bubbling springs in the middle of an arid desert and is one of the ten largest cottonwood and willow habitats in California. I've walked the trails there and had a Cooper's hawk rocket over my shoulder in the woods: I felt the air move from its flapping wings. It should have scared me but only made me feel lucky. I've also seen a hummingbird sitting on its nest. Hummingbirds build nests like Frank Lloyd Wright would. They're made out of moss, lichen, and spiderwebs and are so organically camouflaged that the beautiful silvery-green egg house looks like part of the tree. The sweet, protective mother sat motionless in her nest, betting that in my stupidity I wouldn't see her. Her bravery made me back off. I didn't want to stress her out, understanding if you're cruel to a hummingbird, Mother Nature should go Noah and gather two of every predator to kill you.

One time I showed up at dawn at Big Morongo and was the first visitor to the reserve. I was greeted by eight turkey vultures sitting in a dead cottonwood. All the birds had their wings outstretched, warming up in the morning sun. When the vultures heard my feet stepping on the boardwalk leading to the trail, all eight heads turned in unison to check me out. Birds watching people is creepy.

If you visit during the first two weeks of May, the Big Morongo Preserve is one of the best bird-watching spots in North America. Michael and I visited then. He had already mocked me as Miss Jane Hathaway, the bird-watching spinster on *The Beverly Hillbillies*. So when we parked our car and saw a group of gray-haired, baseball-capped birder ladies lugging around huge, unwieldy spotting telescopes, I thought, "Okay, this might be a dud."

So we walked over to Covington Park, a local town park that borders the reserve. I always check out that particular park for vermilion flycatchers since that's where I always see them. The bird is the size of a sparrow, but the males have iridescent fiery-red plumage that makes neon signs look drab. Vermilion flycatchers are usually easy to spot because they sit on the end of a branch waiting for a bug to pass; then they loop out, feast, and return to their tree. They're lazy eagles that won't shop for dinner—but want it delivered.

The birder biddies were checking out the park too. We had a great view of a vermilion, and in the same tree, I spotted my first lazuli bunting, a bright-blue bird with a white breast topped off with a rusty orange collar. Then in a neighboring tree, I saw a hooded oriole, a vibrantly orange bird. The best part was that the three birds were spotted by Michael, who was using my binoculars. Seeing any one of those birds would have been fantastic—but seeing all three was Mother Nature spoiling her children.

I was flying as we hiked the rest of the refuge. I kept my eyes up, scanning the trees and sky, hoping to see another avian treat—perhaps an out-of-range California condor. Michael suddenly shouted, "Watch out!" Looking down at the ground, I almost stepped on a three-foot-long California king snake, a gorgeous brown-and-cream ringed reptile. It's the only snake I've ever spotted at the reserve. And it's a good omen since they eat rattlesnakes, and if you see one, venomous serpents are probably out of rattling range. It was the capper to our visit: three great birds and a spectacular snake in fifteen minutes.

For years, I thought I had a Thoreauvian glimmer of insight into Mother Nature, but a voyage to the Galápagos Islands revealed that she would probably never be fully comprehensible—just like my own mother. The trip was two months after I was officially diagnosed with ALS. I'd been offered a job performing stand-up comedy on a small gay cruise with eighty-five passengers. At that point, I occasionally sounded drunk. So before I started my set, I had to announce that I had a neurological problem and hadn't been drinking. Each passenger paid five grand for this trip, and while I felt unlucky about getting ALS, I gloated that I was able to bring Michael for free.

The comic who had performed on this trip the previous year advised us to snorkel every time it was offered. Michael loves to swim, and he readily agreed to this plan. Our days in the Galápagos were vigorous and restful. There was a morning hike or snorkel. Then we returned to the ship for lunch, often made more leisurely with a beer. In the afternoon there was a hike, each time on a different island. And then we returned to the ship for a long dinner with wine. Before bed, there would be stargazing on the top of the ship with one of the ship's naturalists. Looking up at stars from the middle of the ocean makes you contemplate how electric lighting has made our lives dimmer—although looking down into the water illuminated by the ship's lights and watching the shadowy forms of hammerhead sharks was thrilling.

Visiting the biggest town in the Galápagos, Puerto Ayora, we saw evolution in action. On the other islands, the iguanas ignored humans and remained motionless like scaly black rocks with eyes. Michael and I walked out on a dock and noticed the iguanas scampering to get out of our way. Then we saw a boy on his bike deliberately riding over the lizards' tails. Increased intelligence has probably always been due to figuring out how to avoid assholes.

Our first morning involved a visit to Española Island to see waved albatrosses. These are large birds: three feet high with a seven-foot wingspan. We walked through their nesting grounds and observed their courtship rituals. The couples perform elaborate head bobbing and weaving, followed by a rapid bill-clacking slap fight. It appeared that the couples were having a dispute, which is probably what an albatross would think if it observed human courtship rituals. The birds weren't afraid of our intrusion, and their display of ignorance was more empowering than distressing.

The animals of the Galápagos don't fear humans, which is insane since nineteenth-century whalers stocked up on the islands' tortoises for provisions. The reptiles could survive for months on ships without being fed or given water. (Not giving them water! Moby Dick was only meting out animal justice by killing Captain Ahab and sinking the *Pequod*.)

What made me happiest on the Galápagos trip was how much Michael enjoyed the animals. The contented, unspooked critters in the Galápagos make you believe they love hanging out with you as much as you enjoy seeing them. We stood in shallow water, and a tiny Galápagos penguin zipped by our feet. We watched a sea turtle calmly chewing seaweed underwater while we snorkeled a foot away. After a hike, Michael spotted a huge sea turtle basking on the surface of the ocean. Then we turned our heads and saw a chorus line of blue-footed boobies feed by dive-bombing into the sea. We saw a chocolate chip starfish, which looks exactly like an unbaked cookie. We walked right up to a fierce-looking dark-brown Galápagos hawk whose yellow and dark gray beak sneered at all the gawking tourists. We were also horrified when our naturalist showed us a beach entirely inhabited by lurking stingrays. We did have a gay beach afternoon on another island. A nearby pond had three flamingoes more elaborately posed than any of the handsome muscle boys from our ship. On our last day, we saw our first Galápagos tortoises. Walking through a forest seeing these giants was like bumping into a stegosaurus on a hike.

Even the plants were riveting. There's a species of prickly pear cactus native to the Galápagos that looks like a tree. It has a bark-covered trunk crowned with thorny green pads. There were islands with prickly pear forests that made me think Mother Nature is warning: I could have made every forest this uninviting—but I didn't.

Our most captivating encounter with a wild animal in the Galápagos was on a morning snorkel around a small volcanic islet—a rock that stuck out of the sea. Since it had no shores, we felt we were swimming perilously in the middle of the ocean. Michael and I were joined by a Galápagos sea lion, which should be renamed the Galápagos sea dog; he definitely wanted to play. Swimming around and between us for most of our snorkel, he then stopped for a moment underwater—remaining motionless, staring at us. We stopped moving too. It was a kindred-mammal moment with three creatures sharing their delight in each other. His expression really seemed to say, "Love you guys," and our buoyant expressions must have conveyed how much we loved him too. I got an extra kick out of our playdate with the sea lion since Michael couldn't stop talking about it for the rest of the trip.

Love is a neurological feeling that's also a belief. It can't be scientifically measured, but there are numerous ways to prove that love exists. The simplest method—but not one I'd recommend—is getting a life-threatening illness. I live in Manhattan, and when New Yorkers see me struggling, trying to swipe my subway card through the most handicapped-unfriendly entrance system, someone invariably asks, "Do you need help?"

Without the love and courage of Michael, I would be physically and emotionally dead. I was diagnosed with ALS a year after we started dating. When I told Michael the news, he said, "We'll get through this."

Really, I wouldn't have blamed him for breaking up with me.

Who wants a dying boyfriend? At some point it has to make you feel like a necrophiliac. But I don't accept my prognosis of death. It might happen, but our lives are filled with close calls like suddenly finding yourself stuck on a cliff in New Hampshire.

Michael has assumed responsibility for all our household chores since my hands now work as if they're perpetually giving me a raised middle finger. He gets me coffee every day, which may sound trivial, but anyone who knows me understands that if lattes flowed through the circulatory systems of humans, I'd be a javampire. Even though I have to type out every thought on my iPad, I'm guessing we probably communicate better than a lot of couples. Michael still treats me like a boyfriend and gets pissed off when he discovers that I haven't told him good news—such as a famous Broadway director wanting to adapt *Selfish & Perverse*, my Alaskan novel, into a play. And just like any other boyfriend, he also castigates me for a more conventional annoyance: leaving the bathtub drain jammed with a fur coat of my body hair. In fact, Michael gets angrier than a PETA member about my fur negligence.

During the Harmonic Convergence in the summer of 1987, Michael Hart and I first visited Santa Fe. We put up a tent at a New Age gathering. There were daily meditation classes where I usually reflected that the folks who thought of themselves as wise old souls had to have been smug and boring in their previous lives too.

We did fall in love with Santa Fe. One of the attractions was the old cottonwood trees growing in the city. I grew up with American elms and maple trees, but a cottonwood tree's branches often veer off at crazy angles giving it a wildness that makes finding one growing next to a sidewalk as exciting as spotting a black bear in your driveway. There's a photograph from that trip of me in front of one of my favorite old cottonwoods on Grant Avenue—the tree is still standing—proving that a Nature Boy feels that snapshots with his favorite biological living things are family photographs.

I know some people think Santa Fe's adobe architecture is cartoony and when I see adobe convenience stores, I feel the tug of mocking them. But Santa Fe is a city that has embraced its regional history and identity. An adobe McDonald's might appear ludicrous, but it's a relief to visit one state that's chosen not to be united by conformity.

Michael Hart moved to Santa Fe in 1989, and I visited him there almost every year. In 2005, I ditched living in Los Angeles, and we bought a house together. It was on five acres, a fifteen-minute drive from the plaza. The beauty of Santa Fe is that it's a town-sized city, and the landscape is natural. In the high desert, there's not enough water for lawns and everyone's front and backyards are piñon trees and chamisa bushes. One summer we had a lot of rain and there was an article in the *Santa Fe New Mexican*, one of the best newspapers in the country, about how rare wildflowers were blooming due to the torrential weather. There was a photo of a pale tubed flower called the blue ipomopsis, an uncommon species. The next day walking with Michael and his dog in the arroyo near our property, I spotted that exact flower. This was preposterously unbelievable, but now, after being diagnosed with ALS, I figure the universe owes me some unexpected delights.

Every morning I'd join Michael for an arroyo hike since starting your day's journey by refusing a beautiful walk indicates you're an idiot; or you're a man who believes that starting your day by having fun isn't the correct way to live. Some people think pleasure in our lives shouldn't last longer than an orgasm. They're convinced God created sex to show us that happiness is the length of a moan.

Hiking away from your life gives you a vantage point from which to see your life. You're more observant out in nature. My Nature Boys and I talk about everything: mushrooms, wildflowers, turtles, deer, birds. But we also discuss boyfriend problems, family complications, job challenges, and, of course, health issues.

❧

Unfortunately, nature is easier to identify than nurture. There are no field guides that teach you how to identify the poison ivy people in your life or how to avoid having any contact with them. The best we can do is hope that most of our friends, lovers, and family will be beehives. We'll tolerate their stings because we want the honey.

While California is home to unique wonders like sequoias and redwoods, there are also a slew of lesser-known marvels. The California Floristic Province is an official biodiversity hot spot, home to over thirty-five hundred species of plants, 61 percent of which are endemic species. I think my favorite shrub—a phrase I never dreamed I'd be using—is the matilija poppy. It's a drab khaki-brown bush that can grow eight feet high and has the largest flowers of any California native plant. The blossoms look exactly like fried eggs. It's beautifully hilarious—perhaps the best botanical joke Mother Nature ever cracked.

John and I first saw them hiking in the seven-thousand-acre Malibu Creek State Park, one of my favorite places in California. On our hike, John was on the lookout for dudleyas, a group of California native succulents. John explained they can live up to a hundred years and many are rare or endangered species. When we spotted them growing on cliff faces, John added that rainwater needs to fall off the plants or their leaves will rot. They're strange plants with waxy-looking, small pale-green leaves often shaped in a rosette pattern. They look Martian.

John really made me appreciate California native plants. His yard in LA is a cornucopia of native flora, and it's been included on many garden tours. John buys his plants at the nursery run by the Theodore Payne Foundation for Wild Flowers and Native Plants, which he dubbed "Theater of Pain," a moniker I embraced.

We bought plants—and even trees—for each of our gardens in LA, and our support for conservation increased when we noticed the nursery's staff was frequently made up of beautiful men. John has always liked hairy-chested guys. (His handsome husband, Curt Bouton, has prairie pecs.) I was reading tags on plants when John gave me a subtle nudge, pointing out a handsome blond. The woolly-mammoth hunk reminded us that while we were fauna interested in native flora, a rose tattoo on a hairy, powerful arm will always be our favorite wildflower.

It must seem ridiculous that three Nature Boys live in Manhattan. But I like unusual animals and plants, and New York City is the terrain of unusual people. Meeting one redneck in Mississippi satisfies your curiosity since they're as common as house sparrows.

Eddie is a New Yorker and, like my Michael, has helped me with my endless ALS challenges. I'm at the point where everything is hard to do—everything! Picking up a cup. Using a spoon. Putting on deodorant. Most of the time, I'm genuinely happy but can't explain why, which is probably what a woodchuck would tell you. Eddie has suffered from depression all his life, but our senses of humor fight against feeling down. Many of the people I love suffer from depression: my Michael, my sister, my mom, and my good friend Judy Gold. I understand that it's an illness like my ALS. It's something you have to deal with every day, and there's no cure—yet. (Although nature is the best medicine for despair.)

Eddie travels to Boston with me to see my new doctor, helps me put on my coat when he sees me struggling, yanks up my pants when my butt crack starts peeking over the fence, and assists me in countless other helpful ways. His husband, Court Stroud, is equally as thoughtful and always makes me laugh when he comments, "Oh, Bob! We know you have a hot ass!" while he hikes up my shorts.

❧

One time, on a beautiful summer day, Eddie and I went to write in Washington Square Park. It's filled with massive old trees and is a chlorophyll inhaler for wheezing urbanites. We picked a quiet bench, but our attention was immediately focused on a group of fundamentalist Christians using a loudspeaker system to turn freedom of speech into a dictatorship of lecturing.

We started out identifying with Jesus's statement from the cross, "Father, forgive them, for they know not what they do." But after an hour of ceaseless preaching, I said to Eddie, "You come to a public park to relax, not to have your ears crucified by Bible-thumpers." Finally I reached the point of Jesus's other statement from the cross, "My God, My God, why have you forsaken me?" I fully grasped that one of the most important aspects of freedom of speech is the right to tell someone to "shut the fuck up!"

Unfortunately, my disease was at the stage where I was still under the delusion that I could talk and be comprehensible. I told Eddie, who still understood me in bits, that we needed to tell them off. He agreed. We stood up and walked over to the young group of "Christians" who seemed not to understand that sometimes saving your soul means having an afternoon free of thoughts about your afterlife.

Eddie told me later it made him sad that the leader of the group couldn't understand when I told him we were already in hell because we couldn't enjoy the park with their constant screeching. I also added that their message was anti-Christian because no one would want to spend eternity with a bunch of inconsiderate assholes. I pulled out my iPad and typed out my thoughts, which Eddie conveyed to their four-eyed red-haired leader. He replied that freedom of speech gave him the right to preach. I told him, "Freedom of speech gives us the right to point out that betraying the kindness of Jesus for your narrow-minded needs was exactly what Judas did. You should set out a hat to collect thirty pieces of silver." We left the park, but I felt elated.

Looking back, I truly believe my rage was intensified because I was with someone who's not selfish: Eddie.

My favorite memory of Michael Hart is when after my sister, Carol, committed suicide, he insisted on flying from Santa Fe to spend the weekend with me in Los Angeles. I tried talking him out of buying an expensive last-minute plane ticket, but Michael knew me better than I did. I was a wreck—this was the worst thing to happen to me—and I didn't understand my own devastation.

A few months later, I got a phone call from my telephone company that they were going to turn off my phone unless I paid my overdue bill. That had never happened to me before. I had a television-writing job and was making good money. That was when I realized: I've been depressed. I'm not prone to melancholy and hadn't understood that seeing the second *Lord of the Rings* film, *The Two Towers*, ten times (free admission during awards season with my Writers Guild card) wasn't a fan's enthusiasm but a desperate attempt not to dwell on Carol's death.

Long before I got sick, John Arnold invited me each summer to his mom's cabin on Newfound Lake in New Hampshire. The cabin is surrounded by old-growth forest where we pick chanterelle mushrooms. John took a small cabin built in 1925 and expanded it without making it into a suburban ranch house. It's still an uninsulated cabin that has to be closed down for the winter. The raw pine of the original cabin blends with the new pine. There's an old boathouse with an outdoor shower that has two beds, and sleeping there is like camping out in a cabin.

One year, I brought our first dog, Bozzie, and remember him curling up in a ball on my bed on an especially cold summer night.

Newfound Lake has made me think about how we live. Henry Thoreau summed it up in *Walden*: "Our life is frittered away by detail. . . . Simplify, simplify, simplify!" John's mom, Priscilla Gemmill, has established a cabin way of life that we all follow: eat well, relax, enjoy the lake, and work hard. It's possible to do all four at the lake. I drink a cup of good coffee while writing and watch as a mama red-breasted merganser swims by, followed by six chicks. We don't think of Priscilla as John's mom—but as our friend. We especially like to make her laugh. One of the things we admire about Priscilla is that she's straightforward. She'll tell you her opinion of books, movies, and people with a New England candor that's equivalent to Paul Revere shouting, "The British are coming!"

Enjoying myself at Newfound Lake usually is as simple as having a glass of wine on the porch or hearing the loons calling at night or having my favorite meal: Priscilla's blueberry pancakes. The berries are picked from bushes in the yard, and it's an easy chore for us. One time, I saw a chipmunk berry picking at the top of a tall bush. He acrobatically reached out for the fruit and could easily have fallen on the rocks below the bush. I wondered if any of us would have the guts to climb to the top of a sixty-foot tree for our breakfast.

Priscilla has a proven recipe, and she will only cook her pancakes in an old electric skillet. It gives the pancakes a crispy brown finish without turning the flapjacks into crackers. The maple syrup she serves is from a local farm, where there's a cash box on the porch. If no one's home, you're trusted to take a jug and leave the right amount of money.

Sitting on the lake-view porch one morning at dawn, Eddie and I saw a family of pileated woodpeckers, which are mainly black with a red crest and a white line down the sides of the throat. They're the largest surviving species of American woodpeckers—adults measure sixteen to nineteen inches in length—and these three giants were breakfasting twenty feet away from us as their beaks splintered several trees. I'd only seen this particular bird three times before—you never forget seeing them—and then just for a passing missile moment. Pileated woodpeckers are like eagles and whales. If you ever feel blasé about seeing any of those three species, immediately look up to observe the kettle of vultures circling in the sky above you.

I've only seen lady's slipper orchids at Newfound Lake and in Provincetown. The orchids are an elvish marvel from middle-earth. They're true wildflowers that can't be cultivated. The wrinkled pink blossoms look like human hearts being offered for transplants. It's a flower wearing love on its stalk. I mentioned this to John, Eddie, and my Michael during an annual visit.

"The orchids are increasing here too," I said.

Eddie said, "They only grow in the two places you visit the most, Bob. You're an orchid fairy."

"No," my Michael said. "He loves Tolkien. He's an orchid elf."

John added, "I'd rather be an elf than a fairy. The elves fight evil."

"You know me," I said. "I've always been eager to throw men who value gold rings over goldfinches into a volcano."

A few summers ago, I had dinner with Eddie and John at Newfound Lake. During the meal, I had a lot of trouble holding my spoon. This panicked me. Was it further evidence of my deterioration? I wanted to be able to feed myself. Eddie wrapped duct tape around the handle of the spoon while I stood in the kitchen. I expressed my distress that I was losing the use of my hands. I started crying—and I never cry about my ALS. John gave me a big hug when he noticed how upset I was.

Luckily, it turned out that writing on my iPad without a table had strained my wrist. However, after my recent pneumonia, I can no longer eat. My throat muscles don't work properly and when I swallow, food goes to my lungs, which causes pneumonia. I went this summer and couldn't eat and still loved it. It's the scenery and hanging out with John, Eddie, and Michael.

But the episode with the spoon made me aware of what I'd always known: my Nature Boys are my hiking companions throughout my life. And so are Curt, Court, and my Nature Gal, Priscilla. They wouldn't leave me in the woods with a rattlesnake bite or clinging desperately to a mountainside. And they won't leave me battling my ALS alone.

John is a guy who went to India to work for Habitat for Humanity building houses. He called me from Italy when he learned my sister had killed herself, and he and Curt immediately came over to my house when they returned from their trip. On my most recent trip to Newfound Lake, John and I went down to Amherst, New Hampshire, to meet with conservation groups about fifteen acres of land owned by John that he wants to preserve. The land had been owned by John's grandparents. All good things, but you know what I thought was the most charitable thing John did during our outing? We stopped for lunch at a great burrito place Priscilla had recommended. A very muscular guy in a white T-shirt sat down next to us. It was impossible for a gay man not to notice him. John gave me the biggest laugh of the week when he suggested going up to the guy and asking, "My friend has ALS. Can he touch your muscles?"

🌲

My illness has made me understand that our sixth sense is our sense of humor. Like blindness, there are many people born without this vital faculty; right-wing "entertainers" make us suffer from their handicap. Perhaps we should train laughing hyenas to guide the unfunny to what's genuinely amusing. Do animals laugh? Studies of great apes, dogs, and even rats show these species emit vocalizations and other physiological signs that are equivalent to laughing. Rats like to be tickled, and a tail-wagging dog is proof that joy isn't limited to humans.

What brings me joy are my friends. Michael Hart surprised me with a visit to Manhattan recently. When I walked into the restaurant and saw him, it made me tear up from happiness. I hadn't seen Michael in over a year. If the same scenario happened with any of my Nature Boys, my reaction would have been the same. Your friends give you the freedom to be happy, impertinent, bored, or miserable. (Your partner needs to be your friend too. That's obvious, but some people don't understand that every successful relationship shares more than genitals.) Even with my ALS, my best friends make me feel like the luckiest guy in the world. (I know Lou Gehrig claimed the same thing. It might be a symptom of the disease.)

My Michael and I recently went on a trip to Buenos Aires, Patagonia, Tierra del Fuego, Antarctica, and the Falkland Islands. My favorite part of the trip was visiting the Falklands. The population consists of twenty-nine hundred Dickens characters. The Falklanders are preeningly British with a fervor that makes you suspect the penguins have Maggie Smith accents and the seagulls sound like cockneys.

This was a trip where I had to communicate by iPad. We were on a cruise ship with a small subgroup of gay and lesbian passengers. Michael was traveling with a conversationally disabled boyfriend, but after spending time with the other passengers, I thought, "When I could talk, at least I wasn't dull."

I made up for having to laboriously write out funny remarks by picking several wildlife tours offered by the cruise ship. The gay travel group suggested three tours, but for me, there wasn't enough outdoors. One was a tour of Stanley, the capital of the Falklands. Stanley is tiny. No New Yorker needs a guide for a city smaller than the Greenwich Village. Instead, I picked a tour of Bluff Cove, which has a thriving colony of gentoo penguins and a new colony of king penguins. Bluff Cove was about an hour drive from Stanley on a sheep and cattle ranch.

The Falkland Islands have no native trees, and the oddball grassy, mountainous landscape is the perfect setting for a community of gregarious recluses. Its desolate bleakness seemed to emphasize that even the rocks in the Falklands must be suicidal. There are no roads to Bluff Cove; we had to travel over bumpy terrain by four-wheel-drive Land Rover. The bumpiness of the ride made the scenery look like it had Parkinson's disease. (Sorry about the disease metaphor. But when you have ALS . . .)

We were dropped off at an inlet where the tide was out, and several hundred penguins were either standing or lying on their bellies. It was overcast, but a patch of sunlight illuminated the sand on the far shore of the inlet. The grass was gray with molted penguin feathers, and the bare stretches of brown earth were streaked with white stripes of penguin poop. Michael and I laughed when we witnessed a white-bellied penguin shoot a foot-long stream of guano from the prone position.

"Jesus," I typed. "I hope I'm never so lazy that I think it's okay to shit while napping."

We hung out with the penguins. They didn't seem bothered by us, and their bathroom habits didn't gross us out. My new definition of cuteness is a bird who can squirt shit and still be adorable. We watched penguins entering and exiting the surf, running, and waddling along the beach. And then I noticed Michael was crying.

He explained that he was happy.

So was I.

Homer and Yukon Island

Will we see any bears?" I asked. It was 7 p.m., not a normal time to start a hike in the Lower 48. We were in a city park, speculating whether we were going to bump into a grizzly. It was Anchorage's largest park—Far North Bicentennial Park—almost four thousand acres, five times the size of Central Park in Manhattan. Far North was also an urban extension of five-hundred-thousand-acre Chugach State Park. The parking lot had advisory signs about bears.

"We might," said Jonathan. "Someone was mauled here recently."

"We'd make a nice three-course dinner for a grizzly," I joked.

"You're hiking with two born-in-Alaska guys, you cheechako," said Brad.

Cheechako was Alaskan slang for a newbie to our forty-ninth state. I understood that, since I was reading every book with Alaska in the title.

"Is that supposed to make me feel protected?" I asked. "Brad, you told me, 'People die up here all the time.'"

"That's our state motto," Jonathan added.

"It should be on our license plates," Brad said.

"So you're telling me Alaska is our biggest state . . . and coffin."

Jonathan rolled his green eyes. "Every bird on this hike is going to chirp 'Cheechako,'" he said.

Once I committed to writing a novel about salmon fishing, I decided that I needed to spend more time in Alaska. My objective was to know the state like a resident, not a visitor. I didn't have a plan other than to stay with Alaskans and do what they suggested, which included hiking with grizzlies in city parks bigger than the average Texas ranch. My qualms about writing a novel about Alaska were larger than Denali. Since Brad Williams was the inspiration for my novel, I decided to visit him in Anchorage.

In Anchorage, I stayed at Brad's two-bedroom condo with his new boyfriend, Jonathan Behaylo. Jonathan was twenty-two, sandy-haired, and handsome enough to deflate the egos of movie stars. His dazzling smile would be handy during a blackout for emergency illumination.

We hiked the trails in the heavily forested park for two hours. I was continually on the lookout for bruins. Not out of fear, but to learn if I could meet a bear in the woods and still remain a fan of predators. We did witness a mom pushing a baby stroller up a bumpy dirt trail. The infant was crying and I interpreted his wailing as "What about the fucking bears?" I was more focused on the observation that the midnight sun gives an extra day of vacation all summer. Everyone in Anchorage seemed buzzed by solar power. It astonished me to see a guy in Delaney Park playing Frisbee catch with his dog at eleven thirty at night. After our bear-free jaunt, we had dinner at a restaurant, sitting outside to watch the midnight sunset. That night revealed to me why I love Alaska. Every summer day in Alaska is a hulking bodybuilder twice the size of normal days. I've always loved bodybuilders so of course it increased my passion for Alaska.

Over dinner, Brad told me that the upcoming weekend we were going to drive down to his hometown of Homer. "My friend Jen has invited us to her family's Fourth of July get-together on Yukon Island. Jen's bisexual so we won't be the only queers." It sounded great since both Homer and Yukon Island would be new Alaska destinations for me.

Homer is a four-hour drive from Anchorage. We left after Brad finished work at the Japanese consulate, hitting the road at 7 p.m. Just south of the city, we stopped at Potter Marsh. Boardwalks were built over the wetland, where we touristed and saw sandhill cranes and big salmon swimming up Rabbit Creek. Those two animals in Alaska are like rats and roaches in Manhattan; it's almost impossible not to see them.

After we left Potter Marsh, we drove in the land of midnight sunset. Looking at Alaska's mountains, forests, rivers, and ocean makes Americans feel adventurous, but it's a self-deluded ruse. You know bears, moose, and wolves live there, but you're looking from the safety of a car. Unless you get out and hike in the wilderness, you have the pioneer spirit of a throw pillow.

When we got to Homer, Brad pulled his pickup over in a sightseeing spot. I thought the view made the rest of Alaska look dowdy. Homer is on the north shore of Katchemak Bay. Across the water is a range of snow-covered peaks. A unique geographical feature of the town is the Homer Spit, a four and a half mile narrow peninsula that juts into the bay. The front yard of Homer's five thousand residents is Kachemak Bay and the four-hundred-thousand-acre Kachemak Bay State Park, Alaska's first state park.

In Homer, I've discovered the view walks into your life. I once stayed with Brad in a tract neighborhood of ranch houses that was anything but suburban. One afternoon, we had to brake our car and wait for three sandhill cranes to cross the road. As we watched them daintily lifting their long legs to walk from lawn to lawn, I felt my life was no longer a home movie, but a *National Geographic Special.*

For my first visit, Brad insisted we had to stop at the Salty Dawg. It's a historic saloon on the Homer Spit that opened in 1957, built out of frontier buildings, including part of Brad's grandfather's fishing shack. The bar was packed. Travel Tip: have a beer there in the late afternoon. It's the perfect reward after a day's hiking. You'll get to appreciate the dollar bills pinned to every wall surface. Even the graffiti-incised, lacquered wood tables struck me as beautiful, not defaced.

The three of us camped for the night in the living room of a straight couple, friends of Brad's. The next morning we left early to meet Jen Bersch. At a neighbor's house, looking like lawn ornaments, were a cow moose and her calf munching bushes. "This is my first moose sighting," I said.

"Was popping your moose cherry enjoyable?" asked Jonathan.

"Yes," I said, thrilled to see the meese. (My friend John Bateman suggested this should be the plural for moose. I agree.)

"It's almost impossible not to see a moose in Homer," said Brad. "They pop up all over town."

"Each time you spot one," I said, "you reassess your prejudice that all vegetarians are scrawny."

We drove out on the spit to Homer's harbor, where Jen and her boat were waiting. The boat looked like a recreational tugboat. She's a lovely blonde who owns a beauty salon in Anchorage. She was also the mother of two young kids. Jen said, "Since Bob's the visitor, he has to wear a life jacket."

"Drowning is the best souvenir you could bring from Alaska," I said. "Your family and friends will never forget it."

Seeing her standing alongside handsome Brad and Jonathan, I was starting to think a tour guide should point out that Alaska's gay and lesbian scenery was worth the trip.

"Bob's a bird nerd so if a puffin or eagle flies by, he'll want to stop and stare," said Brad.

Jen looked at me with my binoculars hanging around my neck. "I know how to please a bird nerd," she said.

She expertly guided our boat toward Yukon Island with a detour to see an island called Sixty-Foot Rock. It gave me my first view of tufted puffins, and then Jen drolly said, "We locals call this Bird Shit Rock." There was a click inside me and I knew Jen and I would become friends. She visited me when I lived in Los Angeles, and I've seen her every time I've visited Anchorage.

Yukon Island is the largest island in Kachemak Bay and as we approached it, the mile-wide retreat seemed to be a gigantic new species of green-and-brown whale coming up for a breath. As we pulled up to the island's beach, I saw a small, red-painted, metal-roofed house in front of a huge, beautiful, unpainted board house with lots of windows. Towering Sitka spruce trees stood behind the big house. "Let's go see my mom," said Jen as we unloaded our tents and sleeping bags from the boat. We climbed stairs and dropped our camping supplies at the red house, which was Jen's. Then we climbed more stairs overgrown with bushes blocking the sunlight. The stairs ended at a porch, where we glanced at a magnificent view that beckoned me to sit there for the rest of my life.

I remembered as we stood in the sunny living room that when I had mentioned our visit to Vic Carlson, the retired judge who was an old friend of Brad's and a new great friend of mine, he told me he knew Jen's mom, Gretchen Abbot Bersch. Once again he told me that visiting Yukon Island was an adventure most Alaskans would never experience.

Vic advised me to get to know Gretchen, a professor of education at the University of Alaska, a woman who could grade a term paper and gut a fish. He also mentioned that Yukon Island was a famous archaeological site, a designated National Historic Landmark.

Of course, Vic had a copy of Frederica de Laguna's rare book, *The Archaeology of Cook Inlet, Alaska*. De Laguna was one of the first woman anthropologists and led an important dig on Yukon Island. Her book had dozens of photographs of early Eskimo/Kachemak Bay cultural artifacts found on the island such as scrapers and net stones. Net stones have a distinctive pie-slice notch and you can see how the groove was used to secure the stones to fishing nets.

One of de Laguna's finds is a national treasure and not just to archaeologists. It's a prehistoric work of art. She found a large teardrop-shaped ceremonial stone lamp with a man rising out of the open basin where the oil was stored. That's the only decoration on the lamp. He has arms, but his face is a portrait with such a vulnerable expression that you feel like you've been introduced. Other lamps have been found and they have animals like seals rising from their basins. The lamp oil evoked the ocean and the simple complexity of their design proves that creating beauty has always been a desire as strong as having an orgasm.

I was determined to get to know Gretchen and find a net stone. As soon we entered the sunny living room, Jen shouted, "Mom, the gays are here!" She came out from the kitchen. Gretchen has an old-growth forest of gray hair, wears eyeglasses, and possesses the ability to make everyone feel welcome and essential. She uses the island to teach adult education classes. She greeted us like a loving mom with big hugs and also like a wise teacher with curious questions. Gretchen had met Brad, but Jonathan and I were meeting her for the first time. I blurted out that I was a stand-up comic writing a novel about Alaska. I had doubts but tried to sound upbeat by covering up my uncertainty with a smile. It's a deceit that should be called a smi-lie.

"You're writing a novel about Alaska?" said Gretchen. "Sounds like it will have more volumes than Harry Potter."

"It's going to be about salmon fishing at Coffee Point," I said.

"That would require a twenty-six-volume set of encyclopedias," said Brad.

"I'm just writing the B for Brad volume," I said.

"The Brad story has twenty-six volumes," said Jonathan.

"I don't want my novel to sound like a tourist visited Alaska," I said. "I'm trying to know Alaska. I realize how ambitious that sounds. But trying to write a good novel is even more ambitious."

Gretchen said, "Writing a novel about salmon fishing sounds like salmon fishing. You don't know what you're going to catch."

"That's exactly how I feel," I said. "I'm hoping hanging with Alaskans makes me catch Alaska."

I had never written a novel and thought the only way I could accomplish it was to have more ideas in my head than in my book.

Gretchen excused herself, explaining that a flood of relatives had arrived and she was cooking for them.

Jen offered to give us a tour of the island. There is a trail in the woods wide enough for a four-wheeler and we set out for it. As we walked among the spruces, I said to Jen, "The first lesson I learned from your mom is that I didn't want her to think I was an idiot."

"When you think about it," Jen said, "that's what every teacher should strive to instill in her pupils."

Most of the island, like Gretchen's hair, was impenetrable old-growth forest, but as we walked the trail, I spotted berries growing in the woods. They were a gorgeous golden yellow blushed with sockeye red.

"What are these berries?" I asked.

"Salmonberries," said Jen.

"Are they edible?" I said while stopping at a salmonberry bush.

"Edible, yes," said Brad. "Palatable, no."

"Try one," suggested Jonathan.

"Here's a ripe one," said Jen as she picked and handed me an entirely red berry.

I popped it in my mouth, chewed the fruit, and was introduced to tough northern berries that seemed to say sweetness won't let you survive in Alaska.

"That's sour," I said. "If a lemon took a bite of a salmonberry, it would wince."

Our first stop was a tiny shack that would be the perfect writer's hut. It had a view of the water and was secluded but close enough to Gretchen's house for an easy stroll in search of lunch. Our second stop was a modern tree house built and designed by the architect Abbott brother. It was held up by four pine trees and we climbed an aluminum ladder to reach its porch. The tree house was all windows and unpainted wood and would also be the ideal writer's roost. Then we visited two of Jen's aunts' houses. One is set high on a bluff above the shore; the other was down on the beach. They were both roughly constructed cabins but splendid summer getaways with views of Elephant Rock.

It's a mastodon-sized and shaped rock with grass growing on its back. Normally it's surrounded by water, but I once visited during the lowest tide of the summer and walked out to it. The low tide exposed starfish of every size and color. Alaska and the Aleutian Islands have more species of starfish than any other place on earth. Walking the exposed beach we saw many different species, but the most impressive were the plate-sized, thirteen-legged, pink morning sun star and the striped sun star, a small, ten-legged, neon-orange sensation. Its vibrant tropical colors are more suited for a coral reef, not the chilly waters of Alaska. We also saw several Christmas anemones. They were about a foot long, green-and-red gross gelatinous blobs that would make scary holiday decorations for Halloween.

The beach closest to Elephant Rock is one of the sites of de Laguna's dig in the early 1930s. Walking the shore, I found several scrapers and net stones and was thrilled. The most amazing and beautiful of my finds were rock spalls. There were dozens on the beach. They were a perfect circle of stone with sharp cutting edges lopped off from a boulder. I wondered about the inventor of these spalls. He was clearly a genius. The skill required to make these tools was the equivalent of diamond cutting.

Later that day, I returned by myself and found a hand axe, clearly man made, carved from a translucent green quartz-like stone that has to be among the most beautiful tools ever created. The experience made me think of Thoreau's friend Ellery Channing, who wrote that Henry was hiking with a pal who commented, "I do not see where you find your Indian arrowheads." (This is a verbatim quote, but I don't believe anyone hiking has ever chatted that pompously.) Thoreau bent over and picked up an arrowhead and gave it to his friend. I experienced the same awe and excitement at quickly discovering evidence of a lost world.

I had collected rocks and fossils as a kid, but finding prehistoric Native American stone tools on a beach was first contact with a world that I had only read about. Alaska had become even more alluring. Our forty-ninth state not only had mountains that made me wide-eyed, but it was taking my breath away with the stones beneath my feet. It made tangible a civilization that had to make tools, clothing, and houses in order to eat. The idea of calling their civilization "primitive" became more insulting given the vast majority of "modern" people would starve in that situation. Imagine having to make bone fishhooks and notching net stones, instead of shopping for dinner. I would die of hunger. We bought tents and sleeping bags, whereas the original settlers of Yukon Island would have sewn their own tents and bedding.

We went back and set up two tents in a field below Gretchen's house. I've always loved camping: I used to do it every summer in my backyard. It was an astounding place to put up our tents. The shore was steps away. An isolated group of pine trees became our pissing grove. Gretchen's house protectively loomed over us.

That night on Yukon Island, after a grilled burger dinner, we had beers on the beach, staring at a nearby island that had several narrow waterfalls cascading down its green hillsides. I looked down at my feet and found a quarter-sized net stone with its distinctive notch. I put it in the pocket of my jacket, wanting to show it to Brad and Jonathan, who were walking the beach. Wearing a jacket in July is a smart move in Alaska. The nights are cool, but it also makes it harder for the mosquitoes to siphon you. Of course, I forgot about my pocketed net stone until I returned home to Los Angeles. Stealing artifacts is what assholes do, but I haven't returned my net stone because seeing it sitting on a shelf makes me happy. This is my coming out in print as an asshole.

Jen was fishing from shore. She didn't catch anything, but it didn't matter since it was ten o'clock at night and we were savoring the long Alaskan gloaming that makes you regard the sun as a lover lingering in your bed.

We hit our sleeping bags early after our long day. The next day was the Fourth of July. It was sunny and, for Alaska, warm. We hit seventy degrees. I woke up at six and wanted coffee. I climbed out of my tent and headed to Gretchen's. The island was quiet except for a whistling, tweeting bird cry. A call I'd never heard before. It was coming from the beach and I crept down to the shore, trying not to scare off the bird. A bald eagle was perched on a tree branch. I had no idea that the symbol of our country had such a sweet voice. It's unmistakably distinctive and I've recognized the call in other parts of Alaska. It was a treat to have a bald eagle on the Fourth of July demonstrate that it's not entirely predator and has a tender side. It was like having an ice cream with Uncle Sam.

I didn't see anyone in Gretchen's house. Opening the door, I tried to be quieter than that trilling bald eagle. When I stepped inside, Gretchen popped out of the kitchen. "You're up early." She added, "Coffee's brewing."

"Every town in Alaska has a great coffee place," I said.

"Alaskans understand if you need to flee from a grizzly," she said, "you should be tanked up with top-notch caffeine."

"I'm trying to learn all I can about Alaska," I said.

"If you're going to write a novel about Alaska, you have to learn that our biggest state is about small beautiful moments."

"I'm starting to understand that," I said, thinking of the eagle and my first moose sighting. "Can I do anything to help you?"

"We have to set up for breakfast," Gretchen said. "If you would, organize the silverware, plates, and cups."

I followed her into the kitchen after she poured me a cup of coffee and showed me where to set up the start of the buffet line. For a half hour, I worked while chugging my coffee. When I finished setting out the breakfast buffet, we were joined by Gretchen's younger sister, Melissa. "You want more coffee?" Gretchen asked. I did. "And have a piece of banana bread," Melissa said.

I went out on the porch and sat down on a bench. I was drinking coffee, but it felt like I was guzzling champagne. Two Steller's jays had landed near me. One was on a picnic table and the other was on the porch railing. They're one of North America's most beautiful birds with black crested heads and cobalt blue bodies. They were wilderness birds begging like house sparrows. To my left was Hesketh Island, where narrow waterfalls plummeted down green-and-gray mountain slopes. On my right were the snow-covered peaks of Kachemak Bay State Park. The calm ocean also enjoyed the views.

Knowing you're in a special place is always a beep from your Life Positioning System. The Steller's jays were waiting for a handout, and I placed a nugget of banana bread on the table. The birds lunged for the cake like eagles with a sweet beak. As I took another sip of my java, Gretchen, Jen, Brad, and Jonathan joined me. Gretchen said, "Bob, if you keep feeding them, they'll fly back to Los Angeles with you."

"The bird nerd would love that," said Jonathan.

"He's a bird stalker," said Brad.

"The Steller's jays are going to get a restraining order," said Jen.

"You'll have to stay five hundred wingspans away from them," said Gretchen.

Travel has taught me that my strongest memories are formed by people rather than Grand Canyons. Yukon Island was the second place in Alaska that proved my belief that travel shouldn't be about looking at views, but alter how you see your life.

Melissa came out on the porch. "I can only enjoy this for a minute," she said before sipping from her mug of coffee. "I've got cooking to do."

"Alaskans eat well," I said. "Most 48ers wouldn't expect that."

"Well," said Melissa, "Alaskans don't want mosquitoes to eat better than we do."

She's as charming as Gretchen, but I really got to know her well on my next trip to the island. Melissa paints rocks, but it's not a hobby;

it's actually the work of an artist. On my next trip, I brought Michael Hart to see Yukon Island, and we stayed overnight. Gretchen, Melissa, Michael, and I had dinner together. Gretchen told us she had gone to a neighboring island where her cousins fished to get us a fresh salmon. Of course, we were blown away by her hardworking hospitality, but Gretchen wasn't fishing for gratitude, she was just matter-of-factly telling us the story of our delicious dinner.

Earlier that day, Michael and I had spent time with Melissa at her house. She had shown us her work, and I immediately sensed I was talking to another artist; it's animal intuitive as well as intellectually rational. I'd spent over twenty years writing jokes and could see that many people wouldn't regard that as the work of an artist, even though Lenny Bruce correctly said that writing a forty-five-minute stand-up set is equivalent to writing a novel. I'd argue that painting rocks can be the work of a great artist and my evidence is the cave paintings at Lascaux and Chauvet.

I also have another verification of Melissa's talent. On my third visit to Yukon Island, Melissa gave me two of her painted rocks. I treasure them and they sit prominently displayed on a side table in my Manhattan apartment. One night, we had David Rakoff as a dinner guest. David was urbane and very funny, but also one of the most brilliant writers I've ever known. As soon as he sat down, he carefully picked up the rocks and asked about them. I told him their story and David said, "They're beautiful. A memento attached to an enthralling tale isn't a postcard; it's a short story."

Unfortunately, we had to leave on the fourth, since Brad and Jonathan had to work the following morning. Before departing, I wandered around the island, returning to Elephant Rock. Right before Jen was going to shuttle us back to the Homer Spit, I was poking around Gretchen's house, sad to go, but elated that I had the experience of visiting Yukon Island. I noticed on her bookshelf half of a large, round, broken stone vessel with sides that were intricately carved. I had no idea of its purpose but sensed it was archaeologically significant.

Four months later, another example of Alaskan serendipity occurred. I was performing in Juneau for a fundraiser for SEAGLA, the Southeast Alaska Gay and Lesbian Alliance, sponsor of Juneau's gay Pride. They flew me up from LA. I stayed at the historic Silverbow Inn and down the block was Observatory Books, the only rare and used bookstore in Juneau. It's entirely devoted to Alaskan and polar/arctic circle books. The elderly, gracious owner Dee Longenbaugh—another old-growth forest of gray hair—directed me to the archaeology shelf. I spent two hours checking everything, not really sure what I was looking for.

I found a 1956 issue of *The Anthropological Papers of the University of Alaska*. There was an article titled "A Stone Lamp from Yukon Island, Alaska." The scholarly paper discussed another large intricately carved oil lamp with a seal's head rising from the basin, found on Yukon Island. Then I found a mint copy of *The Museum Journal* published by the University of Pennsylvania in 1928. There was an article, "A Remarkable Stone Lamp from Alaska," with photographs of a large Eskimo stone lamp found near Seward in 1919. At that time only three of these lamps had been discovered. The broken bowl on Gretchen's shelf was actually half of a ceremonial oil lamp. Only about a dozen of these ceremonial lamps have been found. (I want to write the curator of the Anchorage museum to organize a show of these lamps. I'd fly up for that.) Rising out of the lamp oil are either a seal head, a man, or a whale's tail. Dried moss ringing the bowl was used as wicks. It's easy to imagine how profoundly beautiful these lamps would be when lit. Finding those bulletins made me decide to make my Alaskan fisherman character an archaeologist.

My visits to Yukon Island turned me into an amateur archaeologist. The next summer I was performing in Ashland, Oregon, and decided to visit the redwood parks in far Northern California. The area was a good fit for me since Crescent City, the most northern coastal California city, was destroyed by a tsunami caused by the 1964 Alaska earthquake. It was a two-and-a-half-hour drive each way, but the trek was worthwhile since Jedediah Smith Redwoods State Park had only three cars in its parking lot—in August.

I walked along the old-growth redwoods by the shore of the Smith River. I knew salmon still lived in this stream, one of California's last wild rivers. It was the driest month in Northern California and the water was low, and I walked on a bed of exposed stones. I realized that Native Americans probably fished this river and also that, while most hikers might be able to spot an arrowhead, most people wouldn't recognize prehistoric fishing implements. I looked down at my feet and immediately spotted a large net stone carved with a square notch. I took a photo of me holding it in my hand and then put it back.

I've been to Homer and Yukon Island three times and the people attract me as much as the scenery. One of the trips was with my friend David McConnell. I wondered if David would get Alaska since he seemed the most cosmopolitan of my friends. All right, I thought he was borderline dilettante. But David is a Nature Boy and we saw stuff I had never seen in Alaska before—even though I had visited fourteen times. We stayed for a week with a gay couple, Stephen and Charles, who had bought a house in Homer. One of the couple ran a gay literary website and the other partner was a lobbyist in Washington, DC. I didn't investigate the lobbyist's job and stupidly assumed he was a benign lobbyist for something like teacher unions. They clearly weren't Alaskans because they served us frozen salmon in July—the peak time for fresh sockeyes. Yes, I mocked them.

David and I would always go to the Salty Dawg after a hike. David smoked cigarettes then and you could still smoke in the Salty Dawg. I even smoked a cigarette just for the experience since it seemed like the last bar in North America where you could still smoke indoors.

David and I were visiting the Pratt Museum in Homer when we overheard a moose and her two calves were on the forest trail near the museum. We shot out of the building and followed the trail until we saw the mama moose and her meese. I knew that if we got too close the mama might stomp us. But the mama moose lay down in the woods and her calves circled around her. We got too close to the meese—

proving we were cheechakos—and took photographs, knowing the mama moose could have stood up and trampled us. It was an incredible experience, feeling that we were hanging with the meese. That mama moose taught me an important lesson. Every parent has the right to defend his or her children. So if you're a climate-change-denying asshole and endangering my children's enjoyment of natural wonders, I will stomp on your face until it's a puddle of greed. That's not the behavior of an asshole; that's loving your children and the beautiful world we share.

David and I visited Yukon Island and we brought the lobbyist partner. We were having a discussion with Gretchen when she mentioned the Exxon Valdez oil spill. Charles bragged that he was a lobbyist for Exxon! I was horrified. Not only was Exxon antienvironmental, they were against protecting their LGBT employees from discrimination. A gay man working for that company offended me mainly for its poor record on the environment—I have two kids who will inherit the vandalized planet they want to create. Gretchen looked stunned then calmly mentioned that Exxon had caused a lot of hardship to Alaskans. Thank god, Charles didn't respond. Gretchen had proved I was a fool for not asking questions about his lobbying before accepting his hospitality. She taught me to never let that happen again.

One more treat for the bird nerd, on our boat trip back from Seldovia, the only town across the bay from Homer—population 225—David and I saw a Kittlitz's murrelet. It's critically endangered and 10 percent of its population had died from the Exxon Valdez oil spill. It was Mother Nature calling me an asshole for hanging out with that lobbyist, and she was correct.

Michael Hart and I also spent a week in Homer, but we stayed with Brad after he had finished salmon fishing. He had the use of a friend's house while his buddy was working at a wilderness lodge across the bay. Our trip included walking Homer's beaches, which are covered with beautiful gray rocks with a line of white mineral bisecting each stone.

One evening Brad's lesbian friends invited us to a bonfire on the beach. Homer's beaches are used more by the locals than tourists. You can drive on them and party while looking out to the south side of Kachemak Bay. Its horizon of snow-covered mountains is a postcard that includes the message: "Don't you wish you lived here?" Of course, Alaska's lesbians are a reckoning force: even the lipstick lesbians can wield a chainsaw. We drank beers, smoked pot, and laughed while a flock of sandhill cranes flew overhead.

Another night we went to a local tavern to sample shit-faced heterosexuality. We were sloppy straight impersonators because we didn't pick up any chicks, talk about cars as if stick shifts gave us boners, or discuss baseball or football games as if we secretly wanted to shower with the players. At nine o'clock, we entered the bar with moose antlers hanging over the door. It was still light out, but it wasn't afternoon bright and hot where the sun is a school yard bully. It didn't feel like twilight either. The sun seemed to be lying in a hammock, not napping, but relaxing. The interior was standard cheap saloon where viewing the green felt on the pool table makes chronic boozers feel outdoorsy. When we left around eleven, the sky was day-go day-glow. This was not a normal spectacular sunset. We were transfixed.

"Did the bartender put LSD in our beers?" I asked. "I feel that I'm trippin'."

"The sky *is* psychedelic," said Michael.

"You're right," I said. "Neon pink and yellow."

"I grew up here," said Brad. "But I've never seen a sunset like this."

The clouds all across the sky were rosy, as were the snowcapped mountains across the bay, but the fairy light also made the parking lot look like paradise. The luminosity of the fiery finish didn't seem like an ending, but a beginning. I felt like a firefly enjoying the radiance of living. It's the one sunset that I can't forget. It was an unexpected philosophical question: what kind of light illuminates your life? It was a year after I had been officially diagnosed with ALS, but I could still talk, hike, and drive a car. It never occurred to me that I might be enjoying my own glorious sunset.

My first visit to Yukon Island was a small beautiful moment in my life and convinced me that I was catching Alaska. I started writing *Selfish & Perverse* that summer.

Finding an Arrowhead

My love of all things Native American blossomed early. When I was in the seventh grade, social studies in New York State was entirely about the Iroquois. I was in the honors program, but a hormonal surge caused me to become a class clown. Disruptive with my constant jokes, I annoyed my young teacher, the overweight, mustached Mr. Simpson. One time he even sent me down to the principal. My grades suffered, and I received three Cs and even one shocking D. Our final exam grades were posted on the hallway walls and I was stopped by Mr. Simpson while I searched for my name. He appeared angry. "Bob, you got a 96!" It pleased but didn't surprise me. Throughout the year, I'd eagerly read about the Iroquois, but after closing my textbook, I'd focus on making smart-ass remarks that would make Kirk Gunsallus laugh. Even though we were young, Kirk was already a muscular hunk. Mr. Simpson glared at me. "My worst student shouldn't get a 96."

The truth is that the Iroquois fascinated me, but Mr. Simpson bored me. There wasn't a glimmer of enthusiasm when he taught the Iroquois creation story. He acted as if the world wasn't perched on a turtle's back but was sitting in a recliner. He taught as if he believed the Great Spirit gave life to men and women for the sole purpose of yawning. My enchantment with Native American culture was romantic and realistic. I read the brutal history *Bury My Heart at Wounded Knee* when it came out in paperback when I was seventeen. I understood that Caucasians were orcs and Europe was Mordor, but I also responded positively to muscular shirtless men living in ecological harmony with North America.

In my thirties, I became obsessed with reading about the Lewis and Clark expedition. Their story is an adventure tale that reads like Tolkien. America was a fantasy land where Carolina parakeets flew in Kansas and California condors fed on dead whales in Oregon. Like the elves, Native Americans welcomed strangers who would eventually cause the dissolution of their traditional culture.

My enthusiasm for Lewis and Clark intensified after I read Brian Hall's novel *I Should Be Extremely Happy in Your Company*. The heterosexual novelist convincingly portrayed Lewis as being in love with Clark, which made me reexamine their story. In Stephen Ambrose's classic book *Undaunted Courage: Meriwether Lewis, Thomas Jefferson, and the Opening of the American West* there's a quote from the last surviving member of the expedition that "the fineness of his physique" caused him to be selected for the company. If Meriwether was picking hotties for their two-year-and-four-month trek, that's a sign he might have been gay. Lewis returned from the trip and slept on the floor in a Buffalo robe saying he no longer felt comfortable sleeping in beds. He also described Native American guys in his journal as "hardy strong athletic active men whose dew kissed loins shiver like fly bothered horses in the evening dusk."

During their journey, Clark wrote about meeting two-spirit Mandan Indians—men dressed as women. I believe after returning Meriwether became increasingly depressed after Clark married. Meriwether also realized that, unlike the two-spirit Native Americans, he couldn't live with and love a man openly. Lewis had seen a world where gay men were accepted and even honored. He might have even seen men behaving romantically. Since all the other men on the expedition were constantly fucking Indian maidens, perhaps Meriwether hooked up with a two-spirit. Once he returned to "civilization," Meriwether had to deal with the oppression of being branded a sodomite, and I believe it drove him to commit suicide. Narrow-minded historians will say there's no proof that Lewis was dude-loving. Another telling indication was that his Newfoundland dog was named "Seaman." Talk about a Freudian slip. What straight man likes to go around saying "Seaman, come! Seaman, come!" amid a group of strapping beefcake?

Later I learned that my Canadian ancestor Nicolas Smith fought with the Iroquois against the Americans during the Revolutionary War. Growing up, my Smith grandfather always joked about our Indian blood. All four of his children had black hair. My cousins own a winery in Ontario on land Nicholas Smith bought. On the Henry of Pelham website, they claim Nicholas was part Iroquois and served as a translator in Butler's Rangers. I hope it's true. After seven generations, I only have 1 percent Iroquois left.

My interest in Native American culture isn't nostalgic. I'm never going to claim I'm Native American even if I'm carrying a few arrowheads of their DNA. And I never will support New Age white guys running Indian sweat lodges. I did a sweat lodge during the Harmonic Convergence in 1987 and the white guy who ran it was an idiot. He filled the tent with smoke and everyone had to bail out.

One adventure was the time my pal Michael Hart and I snuck onto a ranch near Galisteo, south of Santa Fe. We wanted to see a stone ridge covered with prehistoric Native American petroglyphs. Michael told me we could be shot for trespassing. "Cowboys shooting white guys looking at Indian art," I joked. The petroglyphs were amazing! We had to climb the ridge—big stones—and while we didn't understand the reasoning for carvings, great art and beauty is a universal language. There were figures that looked human. The heads weren't so they might have been gods. One had a big stylized bird. Sometimes the carvings were covered by circular yellow lichens. It was astonishing to see that art.

My most exciting Native American moment was hearing Navaho on the car radio as we drove on their reservation. There was no translation and we listened for an hour. I wouldn't allow the other passengers to change the station.

I've never believed the Native American culture is vanishing.

Once I committed to writing a novel about salmon fishing, I decided that I needed to spend more time in Alaska. My novel, *Selfish & Perverse*, would take six years to finish, and I visited Alaska twice each of those years. One trip I met Jack Dalton, a Yup'ik storyteller who made his living telling his version of Yup'ik tales. I've seen Jack tell stories several times; his brilliant use of humor and his narrative skill not only gives a glimpse of Native Alaskan tradition, but I could imagine *The Odyssey* being told to an audience of ancient Greeks, eliciting laughter and suspense.

One time, Jack told a story about a hunter hunting a big fat ring seal. The hunter in the story was happy because his grandmother's favorite food was seal flippers. She would take the seal flippers, wrap them in dried grasses, and bury them for two weeks. They fermented and stunk when she dug them up. Jack asked, "Would anyone like to try some?" His question got a big laugh. I used stinkheads—fermented salmon heads, another Yup'ik food—in my novel. If that sounds disgusting, think about blue cheese. Moldy cheese. We eat that. But Jack also mentioned you have to thank the spirit of the ring seal; it gave its life to help the hunter live. The Yup'ik thank all their food: salmon, caribou, seals. We don't do that. We eat a burger without thinking of the cow. Each tribe has a different religious tradition but one unifying belief in the vital importance of respecting the land and the plants and animals who live with us.

We live on North America, but Native Americans live *with* North America. Native Americans didn't cause the extinction of passenger pigeons and ivory-billed woodpeckers. We did. We almost exterminated the bison because we didn't want Native American nations to have food. Native American warriors are legendary: Tecumseh, Crazy Horse, Geronimo. The tradition hasn't ended.

A friend of mine is a modern warrior. Verner Wilson III is a twenty-eight-year-old Native Alaskan. He's Yup'ik and grew up in the rural village of Dillingham. We met on Facebook. Verner has stayed at our apartment in New York. He's handsome and has a great sense of humor but also is serious about environmental issues. (Just like me!) Most importantly, my partner, Michael, really likes him.

Verner fished with his father from Egegik on the Alaska peninsula. I'm guessing I'm his only friend who's been to Egegik. I understand salmon fishing because I experienced it and I also understand wild salmon is ecologically sustainable. Verner worked diligently to stop the Pebble Mine in Alaska. It's a gold and copper mine that would destroy the largest sustainable sockeye salmon fishery on the planet. (I told Verner he should say all the gold will be used for gay and lesbian wedding rings. That would make homophobic antienvironmentalists pause in their advocacy.) Verner's story (as told to me) follows:

"I first heard of the proposed Pebble Mine when I was in high school. I remember people saying that there was a lot of gold in our region, and that we can possibly get rich off of it. This was after the decade of horrible fish prices due to the introduction of farmed salmon to the world fish market, which devastated our region's economy. Locals needed to find ways to support their families, and the potential mine looked attractive. But the more we looked at the record of mines like Pebble across the world and their impact on lands and waters, the more we became concerned. We started hearing from professional scientists who warned us that Pebble could have a devastating impact on our fishery, and that fired us up to protect our salmon and way of life. After all, fishing is our dear tradition that our ancestors passed on to us, and that we depend on not just to make money off of, but also to feed our families.

"The pain that my mother's relatives on St. Lawrence Island, Alaska, endured also motivated me to fight the mine. Decades ago, the military dumped their contamination on a base on the island. People who depended on the clean lands, waters, and wildlife to feed their families started dying of cancers and illnesses. They had many times the amount of pollutants in their bodies due to the military's pollution. This environmental justice issue is dear to my heart and that's why my aunt Annie Alowa, who proclaimed she would 'fight until I melt,' will forever be my greatest role model.

"When I was a freshman at Brown University, my high school friends and I organized a call to talk about how we could fight Pebble Mine. They were all over the country going to different schools as well. Later on, Pebble and the pollution my family endured on St. Lawrence Island helped motivate me to get a degree in environmental studies and to write my senior thesis about the laws and policies of mining in Alaska so that I could understand how to take advantage of them for our interests. Immediately after graduating, I moved back home to help protect the fishery not just from mining but also proposed offshore drilling in the region. We saw the heartbreaking impacts from the Exxon Valdez oil spill just a few decades earlier after all.

"One of our elders though had labeled our efforts to stop the mine as futile. 'It's going to get developed anyway' so we might as well try to get as many economic benefits as possible. This was unacceptable to me and many others. After reading the book *King of Fish* by David Montgomery that detailed how salmon fisheries around the world had drastically declined or were extinct, I vowed to keep fighting just like Annie Alowa. When I started to work for a coalition of tribes from Bristol Bay who organized to fight the mine, I remember getting harassed by mine supporters. One of them threatened to beat me up; another threatened that they'd end my career. 'You used to have so much potential,' the pro-Pebble support said. Cynthia Carroll, then the CEO of Anglo American who was bankrolling the mine at the time, once accused me and my allies of recruiting five-year-olds to sign online petitions to show others that there were many people against the mine. Her underestimation of the opposition fired us up even more.

"When the EPA decided to step in to study the potential impacts of the mine, I proudly wore a sealskin vest that my grandma had made to each of the hearings that they conducted to improve their scientific assessments. Bristol Bay and western Alaska is not just rich in wild fisheries but is also home to numerous wildlife species. Millions of birds, bears, whales, seals, moose, caribou, etcetera, helped our people survive in the harsh cold for millennia. My sealskin vest was a way to show off the talent of my grandma and the resilience of our people.

"Today I have my master's of environmental management degree from Yale University's School of Forestry and Environmental Studies. While I was pursuing it, I was proud to say that the hard work of my friends and neighbors in the region and beyond had begun to pay off. The EPA is attempting to finalize their protections for the region, not allowing mining that could potentially have a huge impact on salmon streams like Pebble would. Alaskan voters approved an initiative that requires legislative approval of a large mine in Bristol Bay, but only after scientific evidence proves it can't harm a fishery. President Obama permanently protected Bristol Bay from offshore drilling, calling the region a 'national treasure' when doing so. It is an honor to have helped work on the campaign, but it's not over yet. People need to understand that as long as there is a lot of gold and copper in the region, they will always be trying to extract it. That's why I have dedicated my life to ensuring our beautiful region is protected in my lifetime, and that environmental justice prevails for all my friends, neighbors, and relatives from Bristol Bay to the Bering Strait. It is to people like Bob Smith who are enhancing our voice as well, and I thank him for that."

Verner is a heroic man who understands sustainability because his people have understood this concept for thousands of years. We have to stop living like trophy-hunting tourists on safari in North America and learn to live like Native Americans: *with* the continent and not *on* it.

Walking My Dog through the Valley of the Shadow of Death Is a Nice Way to Start the Day

Dogs are the only New Yorkers who aren't in a hurry. Schnauzers schlep, poodles prance, even manic breeds like Jack Russell terriers traipse through Manhattan. Instead of rushing everywhere and trying to piddle on four trees at once, dogs subscribe to the canine philosophy of life: take time to stop and sniff the asses. I'm always aware that Michael and I are shirking our claims to be busy New Yorkers every time we take our dog Boswell for a walk along the Hudson.

As Michael gently leads our dog across MacDougal Street, we're both happy to give up a few hours for Bozzie. We New Yorkers have no problem wasting our own time—posting status updates about our first exhibition at a diner of our naked clown photographs, inviting friends to our Monday night cabaret show built around the Minnie Riperton songbook, struggling for years to raise money for our indie film about a guy struggling for years to raise money for an indie film—but we bitterly resent other people wasting our time.

Though he's a beagle-basset mix, Bozzie's not super-long and low-slung like most bassets, and he's not yappy or pointy-faced like some beagles. He's barrel-chested and floppy-eared with the double sweetness of both breeds. Spending time with Bozzie is always a pleasure. He never tells stories that are dull, long, or too self-involved. He's never invited us to come see his untalented boyfriend play Fleance in Macbeth, and, to his credit, Bozzie has never expressed any artistic ambitions, so he's never going to put us on the spot and ask what we think of his work.

When Bozzie does become annoying, all I have to do is give him a treat. God, I wish that strategy worked at cocktail parties. The next time some writer specializing in gay Neolithic romance novels begins droning on about the hot Stonehenge sex scene in his latest self-published book, I'd promptly drop a rawhide chew stick at his feet.

Boz is a rescue dog. He was found wandering in Sullivan County and had worms, fleas, and a host of other problems, both mental and physical. The green number tattooed in his right ear made us suspect he might have been a lab dog. His not barking at all for the first two years we owned him confirmed it. (Lab dogs are tormented if they bark.) Boz also hates all loud noise but is particularly spooked by the sound of metal banging or scraping, which causes him to jump or shake, almost as if it brings back memories of cage doors. Bozzie has made me aware that New York's a clanging city. People are always opening or closing security gates on storefronts, stepping on the metal cellar doors on sidewalks, or throwing bottles or cans in trash bins. Even church bells terrify him.

Since Boz is prone to debilitating bouts of fear that cause him to plop down on the sidewalk shivering in terror, Michael and I always take the same route to the river, hoping that, guided by the familiar sidewalks, he'll keep his nose to the ground, tracking the comforting smells of pigeon poop, rat piss, and shit-faced NYU student vomit.

We approach an elderly woman walking a brindle-coated dachshund. A dachshund in motion always appears comical, as if the tail is wagging the dog. We stop and share forced smiles as our two dogs intimately nose each other. We're like parents on a playdate pretending not to notice their children playing doctor in front of them.

"How old is your dog?" she asks. Michael admits we don't know his exact age, but he thinks Bozzie's nine or ten. I suspect he might be a few years older. Though he's perfectly healthy and active, Bozzie's muzzle has grown whiter in the four years we've known him and gray is starting to show up in the black hair on his back. I try not to dwell on his mortality because it only makes me dwell on my own mortality. I'm afraid if I focus on my plight, I'll end up "pulling a Bozzie" and have a meltdown on the pavement in an intersection.

On Carmine Street, Our Lady of Pompeii Roman Catholic Church reminds me of a conversation I recently had with my mother in Buffalo. "I've been praying for you. If God doesn't do this for me, I'm through with Him!" You gotta love a mom who's not afraid to write off the creator of the universe if He messes with her kid. I can't say my diagnosis has made me more spiritual. I've always had a supernatural sense of being alive, but when I contemplate any religion it only reinforces my doubts. First of all, I can't believe in any God who's meaner than I am—which rules out 99 percent of all faiths. I believe God should treat people as well as people treat their pets. When any religion says God has his reasons to make people suffer, I immediately think of Bozzie suffering: Would that ever be acceptable? No. Never. And it isn't acceptable with people, either. Who can ignore a dog yelping in pain? Well, God has ignored people yelping for millions of years.

The other dubious argument for God's mysterious disinterest in human pain is that He will reveal His reasons to us in the afterlife. As a writer, I can't buy that. It turns God into a hack who tags on a happy ending to every sad story. As a New Yorker, I refuse to believe in a God who's less talented than I am.

On the other hand, Bozzie has also undermined my doubts about the nonexistence of God. Often on our walks, children see Bozzie and their parents ask us if it's okay to pet him. We reassure them that Bozzie doesn't bite. He has never growled or snapped at anyone in the entire time we've known him, making him, clearly, the most pleasant New

Yorker in history. Bozzie and Michael are my proof that love exists. Just as science can't prove that love exists, I have to accept that there might be other unverifiable forces out there as well.

Happily, Bozzie's bouts of terror only occur outdoors now. When Michael first brought him home to our tiny apartment—the size of a one-bedroom doghouse—Boz would retreat to the bed in fear whenever I walked through the door. Now when someone rings our buzzer, Boz runs to the door, whimpers, and then barks to be let out in the hall so he can run down the steps and greet our visitor.

His transformation from scaredy-cat to tail-wagger is primarily due to Michael's relentless nutjob-bananas love for Bozzie. Michael is not a morning person, and it's my job to take Bozzie out first thing every day. I honestly don't think of taking Bozzie out before coffee as a chore. It's a preventive measure to keep Michael from becoming a grouch. But, even when Michael wakes up grumpy, he always greets Bozzie with an ecstatic, "Hello, Delicious!" Michael's joy is contagious, and every time I hear him say it, I always feel the same elation Boz feels when I toss him a biscuit. Michael can be unreasonably hard on himself in a way he never is with Bozzie or me. I wish he could treat himself like he treats Bozzie. I'd like him to look in the mirror every morning and say, "Hello, Delicious!"

When we go out on our walk, at the bottom of the stairs Boz stops to look out the inner glass door. I open it, but he's too scared to move. I lean down and pet him and he gingerly steps into the entryway. I open the outer glass door, and Boz leans his head out over the threshold to look around. If someone walks by on the sidewalk, he'll duck back in. If a truck rumbles, he'll try to hide behind my legs. I usually gently scoot him with my leg onto the stoop and step around him. Once I'm outside, he musters up the courage to step down to the sidewalk. Only recently did I grasp that helping Bozzie face his day gives me the courage to face mine. I'm terrified I'll lose my ability to walk, talk, and breathe. But every morning walking Bozzie down our two flights of stairs proves that

I'm okay for the day. Every time Boz lifts his leg on his favorite tinkle tree, we both feel relieved.

Bozzie treats me like an elementary school student treats a substitute teacher. He can be bad and act out because he knows I lack Michael's authority. On the days when Michael's out and I stay home and write in our apartment, Bozzie feels free to poop in the kitchen in the morning. As I pick up the poop and spray the floor, I yell at him, "Bozzie, bad boy!" and I mean it. Boz will bow his head and retreat to the bedroom, looking dejected—his jowls drooping like sad sacks filled with tears—and sit and wait until I cave in and come and rub his belly.

Later in the afternoon, he barks in the living room for a dog biscuit. He never barks for biscuits with Michael. I know I sound like every crazy dog owner handing out a Mensa membership to his Fido, but I truly believe Bozzie understands that I turn into a biscuit soft touch if he makes me laugh. He definitely puts on a performance. I'll be typing on my laptop on the couch, and Boz will come stand near me and go into the downward-facing dog yoga position, emitting a low grumble. I try to pretend not to notice how adorable he is, but then he'll whimper, and my heart overrides my head, and I instinctively turn to address his distress. Once eye contact is established, he'll stare for a moment and then bark. Since barking is a newly reacquired skill for Bozzie, we were thrilled when he resumed doing it, which means my "No!" makes me laugh. Once I laugh—and he always makes me laugh—I get up and Bozzie races me to the kitchen.

Michael and I are usually attempting to do fifteen things at once, so on our walks we follow Bozzie's lead and try to find seven years of pleasure in each New York minute. Michael's a screenwriter and a play-wright who's currently working on a musical scheduled to open Off Broadway. He's written and sold two screenplays in the past year, and he also teaches screenwriting at NYU. I'm always working on a new novel, running out to help stand-up pals write jokes for their acts, or helping other friends punch up the acts of big Las Vegas stars. I also teach a comic-essay writing class at NYU. (I had to quit teaching when I lost my voice.) And Michael and I have a play ethic that's as overdeveloped as our work ethic. We try to see well-reviewed films, plays, and art exhibitions, read important books, and spend time talking about all of them with our friends.

Bozzie likes our friends almost as much as we do. He adores our neighbors Michael and Susan. Susan is Bozzie's best friend, and any time I open our door he runs to her door and cocks his head and stands motionless, listening. If Boz hears her speaking, he whimpers, barks, and literally tries to dig his way through the door. Next up is our friend Eddie, who once cared for Boz when we were in London. When he sees Eddie on the stairs, Boz goes berserk, and I suspect that Eddie must be an even bigger biscuit pushover than I am. Then there's Jaffe Cohen, Michael's screenwriting partner. Jaffe is one of those small-dog-carrying gay men. Jaffe's also cared for Boz, and since Jaffe is so besotted by his dog, we've always felt confident he'll also spoil our dog. It's easy to mock a gay man who carries his dog like a purse, but people misunderstand the relationship. Buster isn't Jaffe's accessory; it's the other way around, and Jaffe knows and relishes it.

Turning right on Seventh Avenue, we cut down Leroy Street, a lovely strip of Greenwich Village shaded by large ginkgo trees. There's a pool, library, and park on one side and a row of brownstones on the other. A commemorative plaque on the library says the poet Marianne Moore wrote there. I'm guessing only a handful of people have read the plaque since its installation. The miniscule, hard-to-read inscription and bronze patina make it indistinguishable from the brickwork. Michael pointed out, as a memorial it seems designed to keep Marianne Moore obscure.

We're especially observant on Leroy. Michael heard Arthur Laurents supposedly lives on the block. So far we've not seen the famously opinionated writer and theater director, but I like to think someday our wish will be fulfilled, and he'll condemn or congratulate us for letting Bozzie pee in front of his house. Either would thrill Michael and me, but Bozzie would likely give him a cursory sniff, as he's only impressed by celebrities bearing biscuits.

We always pick up coffee at a restaurant on the corner of Hudson and grab an empty coffee cup for Bozzie's water. As we approach the West Side Highway, Bozzie walks faster. He loves the river.

Across the highway, we sit on the park benches facing the water, sipping our coffees as I comment on the passing joggers.

"He's hot! I love the way his bicep looks like it's testing the tensile strength of his Celtic tattoo."

"Wow! He's got guts—literally and figuratively—to be jogging shirtless."

"Hmmm. Why would someone jog pushing a stroller? Isn't that teaching your kid to be a layabout?"

My judgments, though borderline catty, are only designed to make Michael laugh, and my tone is never harsh, as it's impossible to forget, while they exercise, I'm the bench potato.

We don't sit for long, quickly losing interest in watching New Yorkers using their leisure time to run. It's like fish making an effort to swim three times a week. We walk out onto the pier—a plank of park jutting into the river. It has trees and a lawn, benches and tables, and architecturally designed canopies offering shade. On summer days, the pier feels like New York's gay backyard, filled with shirtless hotties tanning on the grass. For me, it always evokes the Januslike sensation of being a middle-aged gay man. One face looks back and remembers my strong jaw and tight body, while the other face looks forward to a double chin and the love handles that dare not speak their name. Despite my generosity with the biscuits, in the four years Bozzie's lived with us, he's lost weight and looks fit, and I like to think he holds his head high as he parades past the buff-eteria.

We take a different route back to our apartment, but to make the trip easier on Bozzie, it's always the same different route. We cut down

Barrow Street and cross Hudson and enter my favorite block in the Village. Commerce Street curves into Barrow, and at the junction of the two are a pair of matching town houses with mansard roofs separated by a yard. They're my favorite houses in Manhattan, and I want to live in one of them.

I once said to Michael, "If I had a billion dollars, I'd buy both these houses. We'd live in one and the other would be for visiting friends."

Michael looked at me as if I were an idiot. "No," he said. "You'd live in one. I'd live in the other."

This was a comment on my housekeeping. But our therapy session with Bozzie has been a success since we're no longer fighting with each other but are teasing each other. We both laughed.

On our return, when we turn down Bleecker, Bozzie picks up the pace. He knows we're close to home. In fact, he will pull against Michael if he tries to take a different route. Our walks always make me feel how blessed I am to have both Michael and Bozzie in my life. Michael has been unshakably supportive, humorous, and patient about my illness, without ever letting me forget: coffee grounds left in the sink, not so supportive.

A dog's year is a long time for someone with ALS, and there have been moments of anguish since my diagnosis. My doctor wanted to put me on an antidepressant immediately, but I haven't felt depressed. I actually spend most days feeling happy. My contentment has astounded my friends, all of whom are on antidepressants. It's got to be rough for them. Who wouldn't be bummed out if a guy whose prognosis is three to five years is almost always in a better mood than you?

Bozzie and Michael have made me realize I've always led a dog's life. I'm messy and, according to Michael, leave my hair everywhere in the bathroom. I like a routine. I'm content to eat the same meals day in and day out for years at a time. (Right now, my lunch for the past eight months has been an Otto Goodness turkey sandwich and smoky tomato soup from Murray's cheese shop on Bleecker. The staff—Nina, Sydney, and Catherine—always say, "Hi, Bob. The usual?" which always makes my tail wag.) I'm intensely loyal to my friends and family. (I growl fiercely when my loved ones are threatened. When a friend received one lone bad review of his otherwise highly praised book on Goodreads, I became enraged and posted a scathing review of his critic's poor grammar.) I'm with dogs in ignoring all threats of damnation and never feeling guilty about having fun. If Bozzie wants to same-sex sniff another dog, he doesn't worry about some bigoted desert hick named Leviticus. (Many religions believe dogs don't have souls and won't make it to heaven. That reason alone would make me give those faiths the heave-ho.)

Like a dog, I don't have any doubts about what I'm doing with my life. Ever since I was sixteen, if I write every morning and think of something clever or funny, it makes me happy. I'm content if Michael lets me hump his leg once a week, and if you bring me a lime cornmeal cookie from Amy's Bread, I'll be your friend for life.

There has been one significant change in my personality since I began measuring my life in dog years. I no longer have any time or patience for mean-spirited idiots. If you profess support for Republicans, doubts about global warming, eagerness to drill in the Arctic National Wildlife Refuge, defend torture and marriage inequality, or oppose universal health care in my presence, you'll quickly discover that, unlike Bozzie, I bite.

It's not like dogs don't have fears. A dropped fork rattles Bozzie, and I'm afraid of dying horribly. But Bozzie doesn't let his fears rule him, and neither do I. Bozzie is proof that nightmares aren't always a life sentence. He was a lab dog and yet ended up living happily with us. I remember when AIDS meant death and Communism would last forever but, like a dog, I don't know what's going to happen. I've always possessed Bozzie's hard-earned optimism. It's nose-to-the-ground practical and not at all sentimental.

You won't get a treat every time you want one, but what's wrong with going through life believing you might get a biscuit?

Juneau

I've performed stand-up comedy at major gay Prides across the country: New York, San Francisco, Boston, and Los Angeles. But my favorite Prides have been in smaller cities like Santa Fe and Boise—and the one I enjoyed the most—Juneau.

My introduction to Juneau was a Southeast Alaska Gay and Lesbian Alliance (SEAGLA) fundraiser for the following year's Pride. I gave away my performance, but I didn't care. I was writing a novel about Alaska and Juneau was a new Alaskan place for me—not reachable by road, you had to fly in or arrive by boat. My goal was to illuminate Alaska like the northern lights. When I see the northern lights, I think I'm in a magical place. That's how I see Alaska.

My show raised the entire two-thousand-dollar budget for the Pride celebration in June. (Someday my ALS might hinder my ability to pat myself on the back, and that's probably the loss of movement I'll miss the most.)

I stayed at the Silverbow Inn, built in 1914—the same year Anchorage was founded. It looked like a store. My room was small but had cozy granny furniture including a rocking chair. New owners have modernized it, and I still would recommend staying there. Next door was the Silverbow Bakery. They serve great coffee, which gave my mornings a destination. On that trip, I made new friends: Chris Beanes and his husband, Jeremy Neldon. That night Chris, Jeremy, and I went to dinner at the Hangar on the Wharf, where we drank Alaskan White Ale brewed in Juneau. The Hangar is a restaurant where you can watch floatplanes land and take off. Though it's casual dining, if you order their tempura halibut with chips, you'll immediately want to move to Juneau.

These guys weren't cheechakos, newbies to Alaska. I learned Jeremy was Jewish and grew up in New Jersey while Chris was Mexican American and grew up in Portland, Oregon, where they met. Jeremy was an elementary school teacher and Chris was a city planner. They hiked, kayaked, and camped, which seemed natural in Alaska, but I wanted to know how they got here.

Jeremy made the move before Chris. He said, "When I was ten years old, I used to read books with photos of spawning salmon and grizzly bears . . ."

"I was the same ten-year-old!" I interrupted. "I was thrilled by the creation of Redwood National Park when I was ten."

"It was in college when I became obsessed with Alaska," said Jeremy. "My fraternity brothers said working for a cannery in Alaska was the perfect summer job. So we went to Valdez and pitched our tents on Hippie Hill right behind the harbor. Eight hours of looking at fish guts couldn't change the happiness I felt hiking lonely glacial valleys, climbing snowcapped mountains, or gazing at the sea during the long Alaskan twilight. All I thought was: how I can stay here longer? We quit our slime line jobs the next sunny day and slapped together a road trip to Denali. Backpacking among the Dall sheep was followed by a psychedelic weekend at the Talkeetna Bluegrass Festival. Leaving Alaska that summer, I promised myself I would be back as soon as I graduated."

"You didn't give the psychedelic drugs to the sheep?" I asked. "They would be jumping off the mountains."

"No we didn't," Jeremy said. "A corner of the U.S. Geological Survey map that returned with me had the words 'Wrangell-St. Elias National Park and Preserve' printed across a stretch of roadless mountain. I put it up on my wall back at school and stared at it throughout my senior year until I figured out the perfect return: an internship through the Student Conservation Association. I could be paired with a backcountry ranger for an entire summer and really get way, way out into the wilds of Alaska and a corner of the largest protected wilderness on earth."

"Was your ranger a hunk?" I asked.

"Yes, he was. But a straight guy. I did my research on the park, pestered the SCA over the phone, and got exactly what I wanted: a chance to see such raw beauty and to learn how people lived within it. I was on a plane back to Anchorage the week after graduation, May 1994. What would I do after that ended, my parents wanted to know? Stay as close to the Alaska bush as I could. How exactly, I had no idea!"

"What got you to Juneau?" I asked.

"My time with the backcountry rangers in Wrangell-St. Elias National Park had been transformative," Jeremy said. "But after that, I got fired from my roadhouse cook duties in Chickaloon, was run off my little cabin on the far side of the Matanuska River at gunpoint by an off-the-wagon Vietnam Vet, and shoveled heaps of wet snow off more than a few flat roofs with an Anchorage ex-con to earn my daily bread. When the call came that I had been accepted into the AmeriCorps program in Juneau as a trail crew member, I saw my escape."

"Did the ex-con lift weights in prison?" I asked.

"No, he had a big beer gut. I only had to get there. Driving the Alcan Highway in summer can be a hardy adventure, but the middle of January was another matter. Luckily I had an Alaskan special: a four-wheel-drive Toyota Tercel with a melted third gear, no heat, and an enormous hole in the windshield surrounded by a spiderweb of cracks.

"When I pulled into the frosty glow of the Tok Tesoro Station it was forty below. The fill-up would have to go on my one questionable credit card. I pulled off the two sleeping bags I wore and headed into the warm shack. The bearded bunny-booted attendant frowned: declined. After some pathetic pleading, he called Visa for verbal authorization.

"The free coffee at the Beaver Creek border crossing into Canada kept me warm for another few hours. But I was starved as dawn slowly crept over the towering Kluane mountains and Haines Junction. There was a roadside German café with smoke rising from a pipe. I walked in not knowing what would happen. Behind the hostess stand was my salvation: an old-fashioned carbon paper credit card swiper! Oh, baby! Big, greasy trucker's breakfast!

"Descending from the pass back into Alaska, the trees were bigger, the air was moist and warm, and the cute little ferry, *Aurora*, was ready to glide me to the kind, open embrace of Juneau—where a nice clean room in a suburban duplex and a month's advanced pay awaited me. At the time, it was the best of all possible worlds."

Jeremy loved Alaska and had been courageous about exploring it. This struck me as the attitude to nurture when you're in Alaska.

I turned to his husband. "Chris, what brought you to Juneau?"

"I came up here to spend Thanksgiving with Jeremy," he said. "Two months later I moved here."

"He's not a lesbian," said Jeremy. Chris and I chuckled.

"Who started Pride here?" I asked.

"We did with our friend Sara Boario," said Chris. "She was president of SEAGLA."

"SEAGLA sounds like a gay and lesbian birdwatchers' club," I said.

"Chris was sick of the underground queer scene," said Jeremy.

"I didn't come out of the closet," he said, "to live in a walk-in closet."

"Bob," said Jeremy, "the two guys who gave us miles to fly you up here are having a party. Want to come?"

"Like I'm going to turn down the chance to party in Alaska," I said.

The party was in an upscale neighborhood near the water in Juneau. We drove there from downtown. It had twenty gay men and five lesbians. We talked about how many of the businesses in downtown Juneau refused to put up signs promoting Pride. One lesbian said, "We should ask the refusers if we can put another sign in their window: Fucking Homophobic Business."

When we left after a couple of hours, there was an eerie but not scary sound in the air.

"What's that noise?" I asked.

"Humpback whales," said Jeremy.

We listened to their vulnerable songs coming from the nearby ocean. It was like a bunch of fifty-two-foot, seventy-nine-thousand-pound cats purring. I could have stayed there all night because I'm a whale junkie. My addiction started in Provincetown—with a whale-watching tour to see humpback whales. The whales breached around our boat, and I was hooked. I longed to stay and listen, but I had to put on a show the following evening.

My show was at the Silverbow Inn. They had a large room attached to a tiny bar. The crowd filled the seats. I was starting to feel less cheechako and decided to do some jokes about Alaska. My first entry was "I'm from the only place in the Lower 48—Buffalo—where Alaskans ask, 'How do you take those winters?'" And the joke worked.

The next day in Juneau, it snowed. Two inches covered the city. Chris and Jeremy took me to see Mendenhall Glacier before my flight back to Los Angeles. I'd seen glaciers before. Old ice is thrilling the first time, but glaciers are like snowmen; since they don't have personalities, they're basically the same. We first visited the Mendenhall Glacier visitor center, which is all windows for the indoor outdoorsy.

Then we hiked a trail to the glacier. We were the only people hiking the trail and then we climbed some wooden stairs. On the landing Jeremy exclaimed, "We just missed a bear!"

There were bear prints in the snow. Freshly made. It looked like we just missed getting clawed or chomped. We looked in the forest surrounding the trail but didn't see any bruins. Even the bear was tired of antique ice.

I wouldn't be back in Juneau for almost two years. During that time, there was a big hullabaloo about a PFLAG exhibit at Juneau's public library. The day after it went up, it was taken down. The title of the exhibit was "Notable Gays, Lesbians, Bisexuals, and Transgendered People: Always a Part of Our History and Culture." As local writer Dixie Hood wrote in the *Juneau Empire*, the title was called "inflammatory," "offensive," and "too in your face" by the head librarian, Carol McCabe. Carol even said, "The display case should be suitable for all ages. What if a child doesn't understand those words and asked their parent what they meant?" When a librarian is against learning, your town is fucked. Carol had said she was "chicken" and "would rather fight with PFLAG than with religious fundamentalists."

I returned to Juneau a year after the library fiasco. Jeremy offered to take me kayaking. We drove to Mendenhall Lake, which I knew was formed by the glacier. We saw a bald eagle perched on a branch, which distracted me. I didn't ask how to stop my kayak with my paddles or about hypothermia if I capsized. Alaska is so filled with wildlife, it makes you forget about your life. I was either an idiot or brave.

It's a conundrum I often face. ALS is a life-threatening illness—but I don't let that stop me. Is it stupid letting your disease run your life? I think so. I've had ALS for ten years. I'm still seeing friends, going to movies and plays, taking my pals on hikes in Provincetown to see wild lady's slipper orchids, even though I can't eat or talk. So in retrospect, my kayaking wasn't stupid at all, it was living a fun life.

We headed toward the glacier. There was also a big iceberg. I knew that you weren't supposed to get close to icebergs since they can flip over on you. Jeremy said, "The rudder on your kayak has fallen off."

That's when I understood that I didn't know how to steer with my paddles. I was headed straight for the iceberg! I tried back-paddling, which slowed me down. A minute later there was a clunk. I was actually under an iceberg ceiling. The iceberg—the size of a cottage—loomed over me like a schoolteacher about to give me detention for misusing a kayak. Jeremy paddled over and told me how to paddle to get away from the frozen booby trap waiting to sink me. We paddled back to shore with relief wrapped around my head in the shape of a halo.

I was staying with Jeremy and Chris. Their apartment was on the highest road above Juneau. There were steep wooden stairways that allowed you to shortcut walking down the road to downtown. So once we got back from kayaking, I checked out the city, feeling grateful that I wasn't killed by prehistoric ice.

The first thing I noticed were all the signs for the upcoming Pride. The flower shop—owned by two lesbians—had their entire window celebrating Pride with rainbow aluminum foils. Even the manly barbershop had a sign! Pride had lessened the homophobia in Juneau over the past two years.

I returned to Chris and Jeremy's apartment, and they were preparing king salmon for dinner. They were pleasantly bickering over how to marinate the fish. Finally ginger and lime juice were agreed upon.

"You guys should have your own cooking show," I said. "Who wouldn't want to watch a gay Alaskan couple arguing over recipes?"

"What would we call the show?" Chris asked.

"Juneau Sais Quoi," said Jeremy.

"Recipe Ninjas," said Chris.

"Kitchen Bitchin'," I said.

For dessert, we had nagoonberry ice cream with flecks of dark chocolate. Most Alaskans have never tasted a nagoonberry because they grow one berry to a plant and you have to deal with mosquitoes guarding each berry. Of course that doesn't deter gay Alaska foodies like Chris and Jeremy.

"Oh, wow!" I said after swallowing my first berry. They tasted like more sophisticated raspberries with notes of Cabernet. The delicious ice cream convinced me nagoonberries were a northern wonder as remarkable as the aurora borealis.

I slept on their floor on camping cushions, and it was very comfortable. The next morning I had an ocean excursion with two lesbians, Colleen and Di. I had been put in touch with them by my Native Alaskan friend from Anchorage, Jim Wilkins. Chris drove me to their house. I had no worries because I always get along with lesbians. I think of my cock and balls as a fanny pack. Just one that didn't interest them.

We put their skiff in the water at a public ramp. I sat in the front and Colleen and Di sat in back, running the outboard motor. The middle seat was empty. The sea was as smooth as a floor. It looked as if anyone could walk on water.

We began put-putting down the inlet. There was one house I wished I owned. It was on an island close to shore. The house was modern; it was a long rectangular wooden box with floor-to-ceiling windows looking out to the ocean. We got past the house and a raven landed on the middle seat of the skiff.

Colleen and Di began throwing him sunflower seeds.

"That's strange," I said. "I've never seen a raven so friendly."

"He does this all the time," said Colleen.

Di added, "He's our Robin Blackbreast."

The raven flew off after devouring a field of sunflowers, and I hoped the rest of the scenery was enjoying us as much as the bird. We can't just let enjoying nature be a one-sided pleasure. We're in a long-term relationship with the earth and we can't behave as if we get to fall asleep after orgasming, but our partner only exists to service us. The animals and plants—even the rocks—deserve mutual consideration and satisfaction.

We turned around after traveling down the inlet. Almost instantly, a whale's tail appeared next to us. It wasn't a humpback or orca, the most common whales around Juneau. It looked like a gray whale.

I'd seen a gray whale when I went birdwatching with a group of gay guys in Seattle. We were at a marina and a gray whale was feeding between the docks.

"Is this normal?" I asked. The amazed expressions on their faces was my answer.

The new whale had a gray tail and, like the whale I'd seen in Seattle, wasn't gigantic—for a whale! He was feeding exactly the same. He would dive down, his tail surfaced above the water. We were scooting along, and the whale accompanied us.

I turned back to Colleen and Di. "We're walking our whale."

They laughed. I had made a joke, but this was one of my greatest Nature Boy experiences. A friendly raven and an amiable whale. It was Mother Nature saying the gays and lesbians are part of her world.

That night we had a camping trip at Sunshine Cove. Naming a place in Juneau Sunshine Cove is delusional. I was there in June and the temperature high was 55 degrees and it rained every day. Although I'm not complaining about the summer weather in Alaska: the rain keeps your love for Alaska real, not a romance novel.

At ten o'clock, Jeremy, Chris, and I drove to Sunshine Cove, where we would camp with eight other gay guys. The sun was still up, but it was setting. We passed what looked like a swamp on the ocean. "That's where we picked our nagoonberries," said Chris.

"It looks like oceanfront living for mosquitoes," I said.

"It's for the *wealthy* mosquitoes," said Jeremy.

Sunshine Cove is almost at the end of the road in Juneau. Thick forest stood along the shore. Our tents were set up in the woods. Mine was all ready for me. I supposed they thought the guy from LA was too urban to camp, but actually I was too lazy. It felt great that I didn't have to do anything.

The first two guys we met were Rorie Watt, an engineer for the city of Juneau, and an old man visiting from Gustavus, a very small town of 442 bordering Glacier Bay National Park. The old guy was sharing a tent with Rorie. I wanted Rorie in my tent. He had brown hair, a great smile, and beautiful eyes and was athletic and very handsome. I wanted to know more about Rorie but was too shy to ask.

The old guy pulled out a brass pot pipe that looked like Thomas Edison invented it. He filled it with weed, and we all took a hit. Getting high in Alaska feels like doubling down; the scenery is so mindblowing that pot actually sobers you up.

The guys had set up an area where a tarp blocked the rain and a fire was being lit. I grabbed a seat and was offered another brewed-in-Juneau beer, an Alaskan Amber. The rain started up. We huddled around the fire, smoked pot, drank beers, and told stories.

Jeremy told a story about being trampled by a moose. "Chris and I went for a hike on Pioneer Peak, outside of Palmer, Alaska. Only one car parked at the dusty trailhead. As we slowly wound our way up through the dense willows, alder, and devil's club, each footfall kicked up mushroom clouds of dust. It was like walking through a stream of baby powder.

"'Hey, look at that!' said Chris. 'Is it a bear?' He pointed at a clean, crisp print in the duff at our feet. Closer inspection revealed the sharp outline of a large cloven hoof of a moose.

"'No worries. Come on!' I said, distracted by dreams of the warm wildflower breezes above us. We continued dusting up the trail, but within minutes we clomped to a stop: this time the dry peaty ground was vibrating and a deep hollow thumping sound broke the silence.

"'It's a bear!' Chris whimpered.

"'Nah, no sign. Probably just a trail runner,' I replied, too smug for my own good."

"I didn't whimper," said Chris.

"Yes, you did," said Jeremy. "The path had begun bending into a series of gentle switchbacks and when I glimpsed the green blur of movement through the brush above us, that was exactly what I hoped was streaking down the trail toward us. Rounding the corner of the next switchback, we saw it: head down, ears up, and breathing hard, a mother moose with a calf hiding behind its spindly iron legs. Shit.

"Fresh from southeast Alaska, bears were foremost on our minds. Therefore our first instinct was to put our hands up (to make you look bigger) and talk to it. 'Hello Moose! Don't mind us! We are just here for a visit. Just relax, Moose. Hello, Moose!' Chris and I shared a hopeful look . . ."

"You should have told the moose you were gay," I said. "That might have helped."

"We should have tried that," said Chris.

Jeremy added, "But, the moose really didn't like our attempt at being neighborly and charged. That instant Chris, who was in front and closest to the coming freight train, jumped off the trail and into the thorny embrace of devil's club. Glad he was safely out of the way, I had paused one second too long.

"BLAM! I was flying through the air, completely out of control. My eyes were open but dark shadows were all I could manage. SLAM! I impacted the dust. BAM! Floating then violently tumbled in a tangle of legs. SPLAT! Spit out into the brush on the side of the trail and pancaked face down, I thought to crawl away from what was certain the end to come. Yet, only my fingers obeyed and weakly clawed at the ground as I imagined the moose rearing up on its hind legs like an elephant and stomping down with all its bulk.

"I waited, but seconds passed and my sight slowly returned. The pounding hooves had disappeared. The assault was over. 'Are you okay?' Chris called from above.

"Still reinflating my lungs, I croaked, 'No. No, I'm not okay.' I pushed myself up to all fours and slowly started taking an inventory of the damage. I patted down my arms: one sprained wrist. No obvious breaks. Teeth still there. Hot pain coming from my groin. Oh, man. I pulled away my waistband and peered with dread: a raised red outline of a hoof print glared up at me from my inner thigh, a millimeter shy of my cock. Phew! A relationship spared.

"As Chris was picking the moose hair off my back, rustling and pounding noises arose again from the trail beyond us. 'Hey!' Suddenly full of fear again, 'We are HERE! GO AWAY moose! BEAT IT!' We screamed. I grimaced at Chris, 'Did you see where the moose went?! Where is the calf? Could it be coming back to look?' We were in no shape for a rematch.

"'Did you see the moose?' A friendly woman's voice filtered down to us as she and a fellow hiker strode out of the green toward us.

"'Uh, yeah. I saw the moose. IT RAN ME OVER!'

"And we really didn't want to encounter it again. I tried to regain my feet but stumbling, realized I was unable to stand on my own. There was a sharp pain in my lower back where the beast had first rocketed into me. Chris steadied me while I dug through my mangled day pack for the first aid kit and the vial of 222's, equal parts codeine, caffeine, and aspirin. I always carry these little gems from our Canadian friends. Popping a pair, I used Chris and one of the hikers as my crutches, and I began to hobble out.

"It was then that the hikers filled us in on how they first had encountered the mama moose and calf up in the subalpine. They had shooed it down the trail, in front of them, but right toward us. That mama was already pissed by the time we had unwittingly forced her into a moose sandwich on the switchback.

"Luckily, we hadn't been that far into the hike at that point. Within thirty minutes of hurried walking, we made it back to the parking lot. Chris glumly eyed our Subaru and then turned back to my crumpling frame. Chris hates to drive. But he grit his teeth and took his seat behind the wheel. I, of course, spoke nothing but encouragement for the ten miles he haltingly ground through the manual transmission."

We all looked at Chris.

"It's true," he said. "I hate to drive."

"The Palmer hospital's emergency department was strangely packed for midafternoon on a weekday during the summer. The nurse behind the counter distractedly shoved a clipboard at us and asked us the reason for today's visit. I couldn't use my writing hand, so I had Chris write for me: RUN OVER BY A MOOSE. And slid it back to her. She casually glanced at the sheet, but after a double take abruptly looked back up at me. 'Really?' she softened. 'Hey, you guys!' she turned to her colleagues who were out of our view. 'This guy was just trampled by a moose!'

"The inner door to the treatment room immediately swung open, 'Come right in!' To this day, I have never had so many parts of my body x-rayed at one sitting. Painful as it was, lying back in a hospital bed afterward, the doctor reported that NOTHING appeared broken. He was still concerned that I may have internal damage that may reveal itself in the next few days. That angry red footprint on my upper thigh, he explained, was a hematoma, a massive blood blister, and would go away eventually. 'But really, Mr. Neldon, we usually see people who have been trampled by a moose in the morgue. It is a miracle that you are here it all!'

"This was also about the time my smart-assed teaching colleague and Alaskan badass in her own right, Nancy Peel, gave me my nickname: 'Lucky.'"

I thought about their moose-capade. In Alaska, being cautious of wildlife is smart. On a hike if you run into a bear or a moose, most of the time the animal will retreat. Unless it's a mama. Then keep away. Mamas are going to protect their offspring, and if you get too close, you're going to have your face clawed or stomped. A hike in Alaska requires courage. There might be the possibility you'll meet a moose or a bear. (Though I've taken lots of hikes in Alaska and have not had the fortune/misfortune to meet a bear or moose.)

We stayed up until 1 a.m. then hit the sleeping bags. I knew there were bears in Juneau, so I knew not to keep any food in my tent. I just hoped beer didn't attract bears. I got in my tent and in my sleeping bag. I fell asleep and woke up early.

There was coffee brewing under the tarp. I grabbed a cup and took a seat. The rain had stopped, but it was 55 degrees. I was dressed for summer in Alaska: sweatshirt and rain jacket. Rorie was up and sat next to me.

This was my chance to get to know him.

"Rorie, tell me about your life in Juneau."

"Well, I have two sons," he said. "Their two moms live above me. We're a family and I feel like the luckiest gay man because I have children. My parents are Scottish. My dad moved here because he had a PhD in laser chemistry . . ."

A humpback whale interrupted our conversation. It breached right in front of us—for a half hour. I was transfixed. Humpbacks are as big as small ranch houses. The sight conveyed that we're not the only species that likes to have a good time. The whale's frolicking gave us pleasure.

After breakfast, Rorie split—wanting to spend time with his sons. The rest of us walked the beach. I saw my first arctic lupines. They are a Christmas tree of purple blossoms. They're a wildflower that looks prim and decorous.

After beachcombing, we packed up. The Pride celebration was that afternoon. Minutes after hitting the road a huge black bear ran in front of us. I'm glad that bear wasn't prowling our campsite looking for a gay nagoonberry. I was the single guy ready to be picked.

We got home and immediately headed to Silverbow Inn and Bakery for the Pride celebration. We had the use of the six-car parking lot and the room where I performed. Ken Alper had a sign: Straight Guy's Barbecue! Juneau Pride T-shirts were sold. A local bluegrass band— The Fireweeds—dressed in drag and put on a show. (These were straight guys!)

There was a march with about six brave people carrying a banner that said "Gay Pride Carnival." Thousands march in Manhattan, but the courage of marching in a small town was moving. All I could think about was all the young closeted LGBT kids in Juneau's high school. Sara, Chris, and Jeremy had courageously started an event that would help them. Juneau's a city of thirty-two thousand—really a small town. Growing up gay or lesbian in a small town isn't easy, but it's easier in a city that celebrates Gay Pride. If just one gay suicide has been averted, it means Sara, Chris, and Jeremy are heroes. Pride in Juneau is still happening today.

Chris made a pink Q, which he draped around the neck of a bronze bear statue. Hundreds of people arrived. The mayor of Juneau showed up. But the best part of Pride for me is I talked with Rorie Watt.

"Rorie, I love that Paul Bunyan in a dress," I said, looking at a hulking man in a dress. I'm six two, and he towered over me.

"I want someone to call him a 'faggot,'" said Rorie. "So we can watch a bigot get bashed."

I laughed.

"What brought you to Juneau?" I asked as we went in the bakery for some coffee.

"I joined the Peace Corps and was sent to Africa," he said. "I had hoped to go to Latin America. When I came back, I worked in a homeless shelter in Richmond, Virginia, and studied history, with the hopes of going to graduate school. I was broke and thought that I could get a job on a fish processor to make money so I could go to Mexico to become fluent in Spanish. I had applied to graduate school in Latin American history—Texas—and had about nine months and no money. So I went to Seattle, but I didn't know that salmon come back in the summer, and it was winter. A few more random events, and aw hell, I got on the ferry because I didn't know what else to do."

Rorie's attractiveness also included that he was smart and had a muscular heart, raising two sons whom he clearly loved and working for the Peace Corps and a homeless shelter.

"I would've hopped off that ferry because of the whales here," I said. I told him about hearing the whales sing and walking my whale.

"I love whales," said Rorie. "So do my two sons."

Suddenly Chris and Jeremy interrupted our conversation.

"Pride is finishing up," Chris said.

"We need help putting things away," said Jeremy.

After the Pride celebration, I was in the basement of the Silverbow Inn putting away tables and chairs with Rorie. I thought about all the bravery I'd been exposed to in Juneau: Sara, Chris, and Jeremy founding Pride. Jeremy and Chris getting attacked by a mama moose. Me getting away from a psychotic iceberg. It gave me the courage I needed. When we stood facing each other, I kissed Rorie and he kissed me back.

Alaska had become even more magical.

My Call of the Wild

In the eighth grade, I read *The Call of the Wild* by Jack London and loved it. It was perfect timing; a dog returning to wolf is what every boy feels going through puberty. So when Rorie Watt invited me to visit the Yukon I accepted immediately. Rorie was running part of a 110-mile relay race from Skagway, Alaska, to Whitehorse in the Yukon. The race wasn't about winning; it was about finishing.

I flew up to Juneau to stay with Rorie. He has two sons: Jasper and Reuben. Their two moms, Mk MacNaughton (pronounced MK) and Susan Haymes, live above Rorie. The boys had two homes and felt comfortable in both. I also felt at home in either household. I understood why Rorie had chosen to spend his life with two intelligent and humorous women. It was a decision I would make a few years later myself.

I was impressed by Rorie's bookcase. Two shelves were filled with books by Latin American authors written in Spanish. Rorie worked as an engineer for the city of Juneau, but he understood that people who don't read literature are robots.

I didn't realize until recently how Rorie's being a dad influenced my choosing to become a father. Rorie plays hockey and runs races, but he's most competitive at being a good dad. I had visited for a weekend earlier in the year and the four of us played a game of kickball in Juneau's historic Evergreen Cemetery. It's just down the block from Rorie's house. Joe Juneau is buried there. Tombstones became our first, second, and third bases and Andrew Connelly RIP was our home plate: our own "Fuck You!" to the Angel of Death.

Rorie and I and his sons also took a hike in a park on Douglas Island, which is across from downtown Juneau. The park is heavily forested and on the ocean. It also has a big patch of skunk cabbages. The western species has beautiful yellow flowers that stink like corpses. Unfortunately we visited after the flowers had stopped blooming and we missed their stench. For a Nature Boy, it is disappointing to not experience flowers that would be perfect for a zombie funeral.

We had a chance to visit Jasper's school. As the head of the chess club at the elementary school, Rorie had to see if the school had enough chess sets. It was a rainy day, but the kids were still playing in the playground. The children were all dressed with rain jackets and jumping rope, swinging and leapfrogging. Alaska kids are tough. This playground outing wouldn't happen in the Lower 48. "Playing in the rain? Amelia might get wet!" some parent would say. Blond-haired Jasper saw us and ran over to say hello.

We took a ferry to Skagway, leaving at 7 a.m. and arriving at 2 p.m. We grabbed deck chairs and saw why it would cost five hundred million to build a road to Juneau. North of the city is blocked by cliffs. Beautiful to look at but impossible to asphalt. I started a conversation with Rorie as the ferry left the dock. "How did you meet Mk and Susan?"

"I met Mk my first day in Juneau," said Rorie. "She was photographing a pregnant friend of ours. I was sad that as a gay man I probably wouldn't have kids. And I wasn't shy about saying that."

Rorie looked at the cliffs for a minute.

"A woman told me Mk and Susan wanted to start a family. I got a phone call from Mk. She said, 'Hi. This is a hard conversation to start . . .' I said, 'I know.' Then told her that a friend of hers had explained what she was phoning about. We decided to meet for dinner and I made a pie from sour cherries picked in my yard. It was a beautiful pie. When I brought it over, they oohed and aahed over the pie and I said, 'That's genetic.'"

I almost spit out my coffee laughing.

"I had a lot of questions," said Rorie. "We started meeting weekly and discussed every child-related issue we could think of: custody arrangements, toy guns, nudity in the house, spanking, sugar intake. In hindsight, we led ourselves through a great process; everyone should do this before they have kids together! We discovered we were all compatible."

"Nudity in the house?" I asked. "So you Scottish guys don't wear anything under your kilts?"

"We've been going commando for thousands of years," said Rorie, sipping his coffee as if he were describing something as mundane as the weather.

"I lived a mile away from Mk and Susan," said Rorie. "After Jasper was born, I used to fall asleep on their couch, so we decided to start looking for a place to buy together. We also decided to apply for a three-parent adoption, giving all three of us parental rights and responsibilities. We succeeded in establishing that all three of us are willing, equal parents. It's been hard to fit on forms ever since . . . but a problem I'm happy to grapple with. We searched for a house for almost two years and couldn't find anything that was affordable without being a 'daddy in the dungeon' kind of setup. And then their landlord announced they were selling the house and we could have first dibs on buying."

"The house you have?"

"Yes."

"I love your house," I said. "On a corner lot. High on a hill. An easy walk to downtown. Large windows that let in the light. A big yard. If I lived in Juneau, I'd want that house."

"It is a great house."

The ferry arrived at Skagway on time. This was my first visit. The town is an architectural marvel: an intact western town that is vibrant and alive.

"It looks like a set for a John Wayne movie," I said.

"The pavement was done so it looks like an unpaved gravel road," said Rorie. "There are no curbs and they used a coarse gray crushed rock to give it that look."

"Only an engineer would notice that," I said.

"An engineer organized this trip."

"I'm grateful for that," I said. "If an artist organized it, we'd be back in Juneau trying to hitch a ride on a fishing boat."

Rorie led me down the Main Street of Skagway then turned left down a side street. There was a cool coffee joint that served lunch. After downing roast beef sandwiches and lattes—I'm a metropolitan outdoorsman since I like a latte before a hike—we explored the town and then took a hike around a small pond. Skagway's population is 920, but once a town ends in Alaska, wilderness begins. Our hike around a pond might not sound adventurous, but we could have run into bears or been trampled by a moose.

I love places where the border between wildlife and civilization seems porous. I remember when I lived in Santa Fe how thrilled I was to see a coyote in my yard. In Provincetown, I was scared when two coywolves—much bigger than coyotes—crossed the road near our condo. I was frightened because Michael and I had a beagle, Toby, who we walked around town, and I didn't want him to be coywolf supper.

After our hike around the pond, we met up with the other members of Rorie's relay team who wore T-shirts embossed with the name "Dumpster Juice." The name of Rorie's team made me laugh. Taking something disgusting and glorifying it is sensible. I crack jokes about my ALS all the time.

There was a field nearby where the team set up tents to take naps before the all-night race. A campfire was burning. Rorie had a friend drive his car to Whitehorse. We were offered the use of a tent and two sleeping bags.

Rorie needed a nap before his run. So we got into the tent. We kissed each other, something always made sexier while surrounded by straight guys. We napped and got up when it was dark. The two of us ate beef stew a team member made and then watched the start of the race.

Rorie wasn't running until two in the morning. We rode in the backseat of a car until Rorie's leg of the race. Riding in a car while men were running beside me made me feel lazier than a pre–Civil War slave owner, the all-time laziest fuckers: making African Americans pick cotton so they could sit on their ass and sip bourbon.

I felt more indolent when Rorie started his segment—the hardest of the race—running up a mountain for an hour and a half. I was still in the backseat of the car. We drove up the mountain in segments and waited for him. Then he'd come running up to the car and we'd give him water. I thought we had sold our souls at a garage sale as we sat in a car while an athlete ran up a mountain.

After Rorie was finished with his part of the race, we crashed at 3:30 a.m. in the back of a truck that was part of Dumpster Juice's team effort. Unfortunately, the transmission was fried and it needed a tow. Thank God the back of the truck had a roof. I didn't need to meet some Yukon mosquitoes whose call of the wild was slurping my blood. Rorie was exhausted and fell asleep immediately. I fell asleep soon after.

Waking up in the back of a truck might not sound beautiful, but it was. Looking out the tiny windows I saw autumn in the Yukon—Labor Day weekend! The aspens were golden. It was a sunny day and we both got up and sat on the hatchback of the truck.

"I can't believe I'm in the Yukon," I said.

"People in Juneau come up here for long weekends," Rorie said. "It's the Call of Good Restaurants."

"It's dazzling up here," I said. We were in a valley where a two-lane road had been built. The mountainsides were a mix of yellow aspens and green lodgepole pines.

"Would you say it was dazzling in January?" Rorie asked.

"No fucking way," I replied.

Just then Rorie's straight friend Mark pulled up in Susan's maroon Toyota Tercel.

"How'd you get my car?" Rorie asked.

"I hitchhiked into Whitehorse," Mark said. He looked like he was in his twenties, handsome, blond-haired, and wearing wire-rimmed glasses. "I thought you guys would need a ride."

I sat in the backseat of the car, and Rory drove into Whitehorse, where Dumpster Juice had rented a few hotel rooms where we could shower. Runners for the relay race ran past us all the way into the Yukon's capital city, making me feel lazier.

Whitehorse had roughly the same population as Juneau. It had a few blocks of frontier buildings that looked like Skagway. But it also had modern buildings built by the Canadian government: a huge ice arena, an arts center, and government offices.

For the rest of the trip, Rorie and I separated from the relay team. We stopped at one of Rorie's favorite places in Whitehorse: the Alpine Bakery. They're organic, holistic, and environmentally active and aware. You'd expect a bakery like this in San Francisco, but not the Yukon. The staff were all hipsters and one guy offered us a hit off the joint that he was smoking in the parking lot. Rorie and I accepted his hospitality. Breakfast weed and we got sandwiches, great coffee, plus a cookie for dessert.

Our next stop was Miles Canyon on the Yukon River. It's a narrow canyon and the current is racing. If you fell in the river there, you'd drown three miles downstream. The water is a bright green that looks tropical. The pine forest along the river is a memo that you are in the Yukon. We hiked along the canyon on well-used trails and picked a boulder to eat our sandwiches.

"I did some research," Rorie said. "Salmon swim up here."

"Imagine swimming almost two thousand miles to get laid."

"Well, salmon get laid once in their lives."

"They must be the horniest fishes on earth."

"The horniest *animals* on earth."

"They orgasm, then die," I said.

"There are worse ways to go."

"Salmon have tough sex lives; it's the worst one-night stand."

"They can't even brag to their friends about the great fins on last night's lay."

Our next stop was Takhini Hot Springs. We would camp there for the night. The springs had been used by Native Americans (Native Canadians?) for hundreds of years. We set our tent up in a grove of aspens. I've slept in tents in many places but having all the trees wearing gold crowns was so lovely. We changed into our bathing suits and headed for the hot springs.

Most hot springs are in cement swimming pools but Tahkini made their pools surrounded by a small wooden boardwalk bordered by rocks. It reminded you the springs are natural. One pool was a half circle connected to a rectangular pool. It was crowded at the end of summer. Although in the Yukon there should be a new word for Labor Day weekend: Autummer. Rorie got in the springs first. I wasn't afraid of trying it and got in after him. The water was hot and relaxing. Rorie needed it after running up a mountain. I needed it from sitting on my ass.

"People are like lobsters in hot tubs; the hot water makes them give up and turn red."

"I'm Scottish, so I'm a teakettle," said Rorie. "When I whistle, take me from the pool."

After two hours of soaking, Rorie whistled, and we got out of the water. Resting in a hot tub is exhausting so we took a nap in our tent. We had dinner at the Takhini restaurant—burgers and homemade blueberry pie.

Sitting around a campfire in the Yukon made me feel adventurous—for a guy who loves wilderness but couldn't start a campfire without matches. Sitting under the royal aspens with their golden crowns, we felt like the kings of the forest.

"Why is it fun watching logs and branches become ashes?" I asked.

"It's a metaphor for life. We all have to entertain and comfort people before we become a pile of dust."

We properly extinguished our fire, then entered our tent. We kissed but it was too cold to have sex. Our balls were sleeping bags.

The next morning after breakfast and coffee at the Takhini Hot Springs restaurant, we packed up. Rorie drove us to the Takhini River. It was the size of a creek, curving and winding through the land. But we had the river to ourselves. It was warm and sunny. We put a blanket on the side of a hill that sloped down to the river,

We cuddled then were poked with the urge to have sex. Rorie and I were ready for it when a truck pulled up right behind our blanket. We were out of sight, but it was disappointing. It was like being a teenager and your mother knocking on your bedroom door when you want to beat off.

So we got in our car and onto the Alaska Highway heading toward Haines Junction. Once we left Whitehorse, it was wilderness. The green pines and yellow aspens gave me the fake thrill that we were pioneers. But I thought about Rorie in the Peace Corps.

"I know you taught math in a secondary school in the Peace Corps," I said. "What were your feelings when you left?"

"It was the summer of 1988, and I was twenty-four and had been in Sierra Leone for about a year," Rorie said. "I had recently had worms, giardia, amoebic dysentery, and malaria."

"No syphilis or gonorrhea?"

"Nah," Rorie said. "I'd just had a tumbu fly removed from my leg. Envision, if you will, a big pimple on your thigh, except it wasn't a zit. The nurse worked and squeezed my leg. Out popped a maggot."

"Oh, that's disgusting," I said.

"But none of those things came close to killing me—or at least I don't think they did—but my six-week run of bad luck of all kinds was about to start. I lived in a small rural village with about three thousand people. There was no plumbing, electricity, phone, pavement, or many hints of modern life. A dusty road ran through town, a couple of cars and trucks every hour. I was the only foreigner, the only white person. My house had mud block walls, covered with a smear of cement, faded whitewash. I had a covered veranda, wooden shutters covered window openings, and I had a metal roof. The windows had strips of wood across them. They were called teefs bars, for keeping the teefs, or thieves, out. Isatu, my neighbor, would say 'Mr. Rorie, never leave your door open; snakes will come into your house.'"

"Better snakes than roaches or centipedes," I said. "One time I went to Costa Rica and my hotel room was infested with centipedes. Big ones."

"That's gross! One night I awoke with severe pain in my stomach. I knew the drill. I lit my kerosene hurricane and headed for the pit latrine, literally a hole in the ground. No bowel movement was forthcoming. I hobbled back to my house. On this night something was different. I pulled out my faithful self-help book, issued to all Peace Corps volunteers where there is no doctor, and went to the index to look up abdominal pain. The entry humorously said '*see* belly.' Under the belly section I quickly found out how to diagnose the difference between ulcers, parasites, and the eventual winner appendicitis."

"What was the title of your self-help book? 'How to Die Quickly and Influence People'?"

"That's close," he said. "In the morning I took an hour-long bouncy truck ride down a severely potholed dirt road further into the jungle to a small town that had a rudimentary hospital. Appendicitis and bouncy rides do not go together. There were no doctors at the hospital. Janet Baxter was a nice English twenty-three-year-old studying to become a gynecologist. She had never done an appendectomy, but she had done a C-section. She was game and I had no choices. Everyone in the operating room was barefoot. Leave your shoes and therefore as much dirt and disease as possible at the door."

"That sounds like if you drop a scalpel, you'll lose a toe."

"Exactly. They scrubbed up with homemade lye soap. It was called brookings soap because you use it to wash your clothes in the stream or brook. When she anesthetized me, I looked into her eyes and I could see that she was scared. The worst part were the hallucinations from whatever they drugged me up with. I felt and saw my body twisting and contorting, my head folding through my stomach and out the back and back on. They wheeled me in a gurney outside down some gravel paths. All the alien creatures I passed had big distended necks that came up with misshapen heads and they peered over and looked down at me."

"At least you had an acid trip," I said. "I've always wanted one."

"A bad acid trip isn't fun," Rorie said. "After the surgery, since I was white, I was put in my own one-room building, away from the nursing staff who unfortunately couldn't hear me hollering in pain all through the night. Out of fear of giving me too much, they had underdosed the painkillers. My first visitors came at dawn. Gotu came to eat the orange rinds on the veranda. One pushed the door open, stuck its head in the room, and stared at me for a bit. Later the doctor came. 'You'd be amazed how hard we had to cut to get through your skin. Your appendix popped right out.'"

"It wanted to get away from you. Were you too mean to it?"

"We had a bad relationship. It was all about him."

A red-tailed hawk flew ahead of us. We both followed his movements.

"Back at home three weeks later," said Rorie, "I watched yet another spectacular tropical lightning show. As I was putting away my laundry I put a shirt on a metal hanger. I reached up to hang it on a pole that hung from the ceiling from the metal roof in the humid jungle. The room exploded. Everything was in black and white. My body—it was like I'd been hit by a truck. I knew I was being hit by lightning. I screamed as hard as I could. NOOOO! I didn't want to die. I slammed to the ground, knocked unconscious. I jolted awake with my heart racing. I couldn't move most of my body. My right arm and legs were paralyzed. With my left arm, I could push myself on my back, and I cried for help. My neighbor Cidu and his brother came to the window. They smashed through the teef bars, crawled over my bed, and dragged me across the floor. They looked down at my legs, no feeling or sensation at all. Cidu looked at me. The only thing left to do was to pray to God. And they jumped back out the window and left to get me help. I lay in bed, and with my left hand I kneaded my right hand, thinking please I want to have some feeling back, let me have some feeling back. After about a half an hour I could feel some tingling in my fingertips. Later Patrick, the dispenser, came. He ran a small business selling matches, cigarettes, aspirin, Band-Aids, and Valium out of a wooden box propped on a crate. Here, take these pills. These are for brain injuries. He cleaned the wound where my head had hit the ground. Through the night I slowly regained feeling in my body."

"Now that is scary."

"In the morning I sent a note to another Peace Corps volunteer who lived a few miles away. Her parents were visiting. They had rented a Land Rover—an impossible luxury. 'Hey Catharine, how is your parents' visit going? I hope you guys are having a great time. Do you think it would be possible to borrow your Land Rover to go to Freetown? I got hit by lightning last night.' She saved the letter. Back in Freetown, Dr. Zeller was very excited. He'd never had a lightning patient before. He ran home to get his camera. Click—he took my picture. The hair in my right armpit was burned to a stubble. I had a red stripe burned down the side of my body about the severity of sunburn. I had two red stripes down the inside of my legs, the hair singed off. He recommended salt-water rehydration therapy. That meant 'Go to the beach and have a beer.' There was nothing else to be done. He wrote a note on the photo: 'Battle scars from the toughest job you'll ever love.'"

"Did you have a beer?"

"I had a six-pack," Rorie said. "Three weeks later I was lying in bed reading and Isatu came over. 'Oh, Mr. Rorie.' We laughed and I looked up, and from my mosquito net a snake was weaving through the air toward her head. I screamed. She screamed. We ran. Cidu and James charged into my house with big sticks. They bludgeoned the snake to death. It was very poisonous. I don't know the species. I vividly remember looking at the fangs. The snake had slithered up the teef bar where it had been left propped against the window."

"Maybe it was suicidal. Hoping to be struck by lightning."

Rorie smiled and then said, "When I think about how tenuous life is, how unlikely the biological process of conception and birthing and breathing and eating is, I'm amazed any of us are actually alive at all. I really believe that we are all incredibly lucky. Just to be here today, an impossible number of things have to go right every single day. And amazingly, most of us defeat death day after day. I hope that I go on not dying for another thirty or forty years, maybe longer, and I hope that you do too."

I leaned my head on his shoulder. "I'm so happy you survived all that."

"Me too."

Rorie had found a hotel and restaurant in Haines Junction called the Raven. Rorie claimed the restaurant was gourmet. I didn't doubt him. Rorie is a foodie. One time he visited me in LA after a visit to Scotland. He brought me a bottle of single malt scotch. It was delicious. I gave Rorie a drink of my scotch but shared it with no one else. The scotch was expensive or I would have become an alcoholic.

Haines Junction is a village with a population of 589. The Raven restaurant is part of the hotel. We had an eight o'clock reservation. Having a restaurant reservation in the Yukon seems like an oxymoron. And yet, we did.

As soon as we sat down, we ordered a bottle of red wine.

"Rorie, how did you hear about this place?"

"Every foodie in Juneau knows about the Raven restaurant."

Then we looked at our menus. We ordered the same first course: a salad made with organic spinach, strawberries, Brie cheese, and vinaigrette made with champagne and strawberries. Our main courses were slightly different. I had the venison shank pasta and Rorie had the venison strip loin. My pasta had portabella mushrooms and sun-dried tomatoes. Sun-dried tomatoes in the Yukon? The Call of the Wild was replaced by the Call of the Domestic. The food was delicious. As good as a big city meal. Our dessert was tiramisu. We had after-dinner drinks since we weren't driving. We wobbled back to our room and went to bed. Then we made out like salmon that had swam two thousand miles. Without the death part.

We woke up early—no hangovers, since the food soaked up our booze. Rorie and I had coffee and headed for the Haines Highway. Another sunny day. We were going back to Juneau from Haines, Alaska. The Haines Highway borders the Canadian Kluane National Park. The park is connected to other American parks and is a thirty-two-million-acre UNESCO heritage site, sixteen times the size of Yellowstone.

We left Haines Junction, and Kluane National Park was on our right. The traffic was negligible. Sometimes we drove for miles without seeing another car or truck. It's hard writing about magnificent scenery; the words are like gnats trying not to be pests.

Rorie would stop at viewpoints and we even hiked into the woods once. The forest was exhilarating because we might have run into bears. One stop there was a creek and there were sockeye salmon in the stream. We were in the mountains, and the salmon looked tortured swimming up a mountain. Fins were hanging on by a thread of flesh. There were open wounds on the fish. Damn. What they went through to get laid.

Once we left Canada, we had the Chilkat river on our right side. There were a lot of bald eagles sitting in trees waiting for an unlucky salmon. Haines was bigger than Skagway: population 2,500. It has a square built by the military a hundred years ago surrounded by row houses on three sides. It's Brooklyn in Alaska.

We got on the ferry in Haines. When we got back to Rorie's house, Jasper and Reuben ran out to welcome back their dad. Jasper gave him a big hug, and Reuben jumped on him. His laughter made Rorie and me smile. Their excitement made me realize Rorie had shared the Yukon with me. Once we were back in Juneau, I understood that our trip to the Yukon was the perfect mix of Call of the Wild and Call of the Domestic. It's a combination I've been trying to balance my entire life. I always like to hike in the wilderness with friends who can crack jokes about any subject. I've often gone on solitary hikes, but I like hiking with friends better. It's about sharing. Seeing my first lady's slipper orchids in Provincetown, I was alone, but I made my friends come see them. Sharing something amazing is what great artists and great friends do.

Silence = Death

The Education of a Comedian

Lou Gehrig's Disease? I don't even like baseball!"

My best friend and fellow stand-up Eddie Sarfaty claims that was my initial reaction when he accompanied me to Columbia-Presbyterian in 2007 to receive my you're-gonna-die-agnosis. I don't remember saying it, but I'm convinced one of the reasons I'm still alive is that good comedians naturally respond to Pain and Death as if they're hecklers trying to ruin our shows.

Many of my oldest and closest friends in New York are accomplished and brilliant stand-up comedians, but we've made each other laugh harder offstage than with anything we've ever said in our acts. The morning after my sister, Carol, committed suicide, Judy Gold called to see how I was doing. When I broke down crying uncontrollably, Judy matter-of-factly inquired, "Bob, don't you think you're overreacting? It's been almost twenty-four hours."

I didn't stop crying, but I did laugh. I've known Judy for thirty years and our friendship has no boundaries. One time, Judy called about forty-seven times, badgering me not to be late picking her up at the airport. To get even, I stood among the limo drivers waiting at the gate holding up a sign that said BITCH. I ignored the stares and whispers about my sign until I finally heard Judy laughing while simultaneously telling me to go fuck myself. Judy accusing me of overreacting is the perfect example of my belief that comedy is not frivolous but one of the most vital and serious aspects of being alive. Her making me laugh the morning after my sister's death was like lighting a candle in a coffin.

I've often been asked, "What stand-up comics influenced your work?" and I've always cited Woody Allen and Lily Tomlin, but once you start performing, your major influences are your friends who are also stand-up comics. Your influences get you to step out on a stage, but your friends help you develop into an artist who actually deserves to have a microphone. The friends who have most influenced me are Jaffe Cohen, Danny McWilliams, Eddie Sarfaty, Judy Gold, and Elvira Kurt.

Not that my initial influences weren't important. Woody's stand-up act is a fictional autobiography, as is mine. Lily Tomlin is a more surprising influence since she's primarily known for her characters and I'm the only character in my act. But I've always responded to Lily's poetic precision, best illustrated by what I regard as the perfect joke: "The other day I bought a wastebasket, and I carried it home in a paper bag. And when I got home, I put the paper bag in the wastebasket."

Lily was also instrumental in my realizing that I was gay. When I was thirteen, I read a letter about homosexuality in Dear Abby's advice column and thought, That sounds like me. I had recently begun masturbating with the fervor that makes every teenage boy a willing victim of the most enjoyable obsessive-compulsive disorder. While patting myself on the front, I always thought about my classmate Kirk Gunsallus's muscular arms, but decided to test my heterosexuality by thinking about a woman. But which woman? By chance, there was a magazine article about Lily Tomlin in our house. I headed to the bathroom with magazine in hand. A half hour later, my gayness was confirmed. If Lily Tomlin couldn't get me off, then no woman could.

Thirty years later I performed at an AIDS benefit in Palm Springs with the dream team for Palm Springs' old queens: Lily Tomlin, Carol

Channing, Lorna Luft, Jo Anne Worley, and Sally Kellerman. After the show, all the performers took a bow on stage and I felt a hand on my shoulder. A voice I recognized immediately said, "Bob, you're really funny!" After all that time, Lily Tomlin finally got me off.

A great stand-up comic's voice is as distinctive and unique as any great singer's voice. Joan Rivers is our Maria Callas and Rodney Dangerfield is our Frank Sinatra. It took me ten years to find my voice, and I discovered it by moving to New York. In the summer of 1976, at age eighteen, I started performing in Buffalo and immediately got laughs with jokes like "Last year my family fought for weeks over whether to buy an artificial or natural Christmas tree. Finally, we reached a compromise. We bought an artificial tree, but we're going to throw it out each year."

I was an English major in college, but stand-up appealed to me because there is no director or editor weighing your every word. It's the most immediate of all literary art forms—and all great jokes are very short stories. Your work is judged by the audience; their silence is your rejection letter.

In July 1986, I made my Manhattan debut at a comedy club in SoHo called Comedy U. A few weeks earlier my best friend Michael Hart looked through a stack of my 3×5 joke cards. "You know, these jokes about being gay are funny. You should do them."

At the time, there were no out gay comics in New York, though I'd read in the *Advocate* about a handful in San Francisco. But minorities and outsiders—Jews, African Americans, Latinos, and women—have always dominated stand-up comedy, so I figured it would only be a matter of time before gay and lesbian comedians broke through.

I also knew I could soon be dead from AIDS.

Rock Hudson died in 1985, the same year the family of Ryan White, an HIV-positive hemophiliac, began an eight-month legal battle when his elementary school refused to admit him. ACT UP was founded in 1987, and I, like most gay men, was angry about our government's indifference and disgusted with the *New York Times* printing the word *gay* in quotation marks as if it were the final arbiter of our identity. I was also livid that at twenty-eight, I was dwelling on my mortality before I'd even decided what I was going to do for a living.

In 1986, an "inconclusive" result on my AIDS test frightened me so much that when I was retested, I never picked up the results. I was determined to be an out comic in New York since it was the right thing to do, both artistically—a closeted artist is still an oxymoron to me—and politically.

A month after moving to New York, I was walking down Third Avenue when traffic suddenly disappeared due to President Reagan's motorcade. What fixed that moment in my memory was that people on the sidewalk—men in suits, women pushing strollers—stopped walking and booed as the president passed. I happily joined in. Our collective response made me truly love New York. I already loathed Reagan for willfully ignoring AIDS and for initiating the Republican-led assault against our nation's environment. Standing on a comedy club stage as an out gay man during the era when gay was synonymous with AIDS was another way of raspberrying Reagan.

I came out onstage at Comedy U with four gay friends in the audience: Michael, Sean, B.J., and Bruce. Within two years, Sean would die of AIDS. Back then, my friends were all young, handsome, and thickly muscular. The emcee that night proved my thesis that those who can't do stand-up usually emcee. The nerdy comic focused on my friends—his eyeglasses outweighed his biceps—and actually remarked on how they weren't laughing at his often homophobic jokes.

Bruce said loudly with his very deep voice, "When you say something funny, we'll laugh." The audience chuckled, and the emcee shut up. It reminded me of the moment I lost my fear of homophobic bullies.

In high school, I went to watch my friends play hockey. After the game, I was bantering in the locker room with my jock pals when someone I barely knew said loudly, "Smith, you are such a fag."

There was a hush, and everyone stared at me. Pat Connelly, the porky, moonfaced "athlete" with the big gut, waited to see how I'd react. It surprised me that I didn't feel intimidated, just furious.

"Yeah, Connelly, well, there's a three-letter word that starts with an *f* that describes you, too." I puffed out my cheeks in case the lummox couldn't figure out what word I was talking about. The locker room erupted with laughter. Even the lummox laughed. I could see the joy, pride, and relief on my friends' faces that I hadn't backed down. Bill Silecky, the tall, handsome captain of the football team, said, "I could see the wheels turning and knew you were thinking of something good."

It was the first time I realized that getting the last laugh could triumph over the first insult. At Comedy U, I had prepared a line in case of homophobic heckling. If someone shouted "Faggot!" I would calmly respond, "Ex-boyfriends can be so bitter!" I never used that line because Manhattan audiences weren't homophobic, which I regret somewhat, since it would have gotten a big laugh. All comics have bad nights performing, and I observed other comics have those nights, so I never blamed my lack of laughs on homophobia.

The emcee introduced me, and I told a few jokes to establish credibility with the crowd before I said, "I come from a very conservative family—my dad's a state trooper—and it wasn't easy telling my parents that I was gay. I made my carefully worded announcement at Thanksgiving. I said, 'Mom, would you please pass the gravy to a homosexual?'" (Years later when I appeared on *The Joan Rivers Show*, Joan added the brilliant tagline, "She passed it to my father.") The entire room laughed. I followed with another gay one-liner: "My high school had a Head Start program for homosexuals; it was called 'Drama Club.'" The room laughed louder, and I ended my set to enthusiastic applause. When I walked offstage, the two owners of the bar, both straight guys, came over and complimented me. They'd never done that before.

I became a regular performer at Comedy U, and it was there that I met Danny McWilliams. While Danny wasn't officially out, his signature bit was an impression of Bette Davis in *The Wizard of Oz*. His opening line, as he mimed taking a drag on a cigarette, was "Toto!" each *o* elongated. "I have a feeling we're not in Kansas anymore!" Danny spoke with Bette's signature staccato pronunciation where each word sounded as if she bit it out of a dictionary.

In 1987, Danny and I began performing together at gay and lesbian shows in the East Village (put together by a self-proclaimed straight comic) along with lesbian comics Reno and Sara Cytron.

I'd heard about Jaffe Cohen from Danny and first met him on the night of the stock market crash of 1987 at the Crow Bar in the East Village. The show was canceled. No one wanted to splurge on a three-dollar cover during a financial calamity, but Jaffe and I were curious about each other's material and performed for one another in the empty club. Later, we admitted we were relieved that each of us found the other funny. It was the first indication of how being funny was always the priority for Danny, Jaffe, and me.

Over the next year, the three of us performed at occasional East Village gigs with terrible names like "Fruit and Fiber" until the summer of 1988, when Jaffe was approached by Helene Kelly, the manager of the Duplex, about putting together a show for two weekends in September.

Jaffe wanted to do an all-guy bill with Danny and me. We immediately agreed but needed a name for our show. Since personal ads were a big phenomenon then, one of us suggested parodying Single Gay White Male with Funny Gay White Males. (We quickly dropped white when we realized it sounded racist.)

The Duplex at 55 Grove Street had been a cabaret since the late fifties—Woody and Joan had both performed there—but by 1988, it had the battered appearance and aroma of an ashtray full of cigarette butts floating in spilled beer. There was a dingy piano bar on the first floor and a dank sixty-seat cabaret on the second, where we performed. It had a tiny, narrow dressing room (ironically the size of a closet), and the two of us who weren't performing would wait and listen while the third did his set.

Our first shows got a rave review in *Backstage*—getting an unsolicited review in New York was as rare then as it is now—and the Duplex booked us for four weeks in November, then for all of February. Laurie Stone of the *Village Voice* did a full-page profile and review of our show, which resulted in us being booked every weekend for the next three years. We became a minor—but real—phenomenon in New York, attracting audiences that included gay celebrities such as Vito Russo, David Feinberg (he interviewed us at his apartment), Charles Ludlam, and Quentin Crisp. Laurie had noticed something significant during our interview: "The guys effortlessly finish each other's sentences."

Our close friendship developed slowly. At first, Jaffe annoyed me. In restaurants he'd pester our waiter to change his order, bring him more water, or ask if the chef could chew his food because he was tired. Meanwhile, Danny cursed with a vehemence that I found poetic and shocking. One time, when we were discussing the "God Hates Fags" reverend, Fred Phelps, Danny burst out, "With all his bad karma do you know what he's coming back as? He's coming back as a turd dropping from a fucking rat's ass. No. You know what? He's going to come back as a crab crawling on the balls of a cockroach! No, wait a minute. This is better. No, for his next one thousand incarnations that sick fuck will come back as a fucking dingleberry piece of shit, hanging from a crab's ass, while the crab is sucking on a rat's balls. That's what he's coming back as!" (This is a verbatim quote as it's the one time I immediately wrote down one of Danny's rants in my writing journal.)

Later, Jaffe admitted that he didn't know how to behave in restaurants since his family never ate in them, and Danny soon completely converted Jaffe and me into believing that his foulmouthed diatribes were actually the most courteous responses you could make to assholes like Reverend Phelps.

It soon became apparent the three of us shared an identical comic sensibility and also shared the same values. One time at a sketch comedy show, we quickly discovered the group wasn't funny except for one woman who was hysterical. Watching in the dark, I noticed she made all three of us laugh out loud at exactly the same times.

One of the benefits of being among the first dozen or so openly gay stand-ups was that our lives were virgin territory; it was like discovering that you were the first person to tell a mother-in-law joke. Eventually we all developed material about being gay kids: Jaffe performed a brilliant bit about how to be a sissy in gym class; I did jokes about gay boys playing with dolls. "Bobby, don't play with Barbie. I want you to play with blond, rippling, muscular Hercules!" And Danny did a hilarious book report bit about being a fifth-grade queen reading a biography of Judy Garland: "They gave her pills to wake up and pills to sleep! What they did to her!"

We always went out to dinner after our shows, and while eating we frequently said something funny. There was a mutual competitiveness, aligned with a shared drive to make a good show better.

One night, Danny told us how he'd witnessed a fan approach Lauren Bacall, who was starring on Broadway. "Oh, Miss Bacall, I'd love to see more of you!" To which she barked, "Come to the show!" Then Danny ad-libbed, "Can you imagine her answering machine? 'Hello, this is Lauren Bacall. HOW THE HELL DID YOU GET MY NUMBER?'"

That was the first of many times when I said, "Put it in the act." We repeatedly proved Picasso's maxim: "Good artists copy. Great artists steal," which means that great stand-ups gladly accept a better punch line for a joke.

We also ran new bits by each other, and when something got two thumbs-up, it usually worked. We each had our strengths. Jaffe was a genius in using his body to sell a joke. His sissy-in-gym-class routine included a reenactment of a bored gay nerd staring at his fingernails during a volleyball game, momentarily distracted as the ball sailed over his head. I especially loved the joke about a friend who was so gay that his driver's license picture was taken over the shoulder. Jaffe would sharply twist his head to illustrate the hilarious posture of the big queen. Danny was brilliant at bringing comic characters to life. He had worked at a deli counter as a teenager, and his portrayal of an imperious New York City harridan demanding that he slice her ham order thinner was Lily Tomlin sharp. "I'm next! I'm next! I'M NEXT!" she shouted viciously, elbowing her way to the counter, before muttering, "Now what do I want?"

Danny was also gifted in mimicking vomiting cats, squeaky clothes-lines, and vacuum cleaners. My strength was my ear for a punch line. I believe a joke should be subject to the same rules of all prose writing, no wasted or imprecise words. One example from my act: "In college, I experimented with heterosexuality. I slept with a straight guy. I was really drunk." Setup, punch line, and tag. Jaffe and Danny played around with their punch lines, and I would browbeat them into doing what I regarded as the correct version.

Danny and Jaffe's artistry changed my act. Danny's characters made me add a quick one-paragraph portrayal of a gay priest, Father Mary Louise, hearing confession—"For your penance, watch *The Ten Commandments* ten times. Wasn't Anne Baxter terrible?"—while Jaffe's mugging inspired me to physically act out a punch line. I do a joke about how my partner, Michael, is Jewish, and we celebrate both holiday traditions. "At Christmas, we set up a Nativity scene, but all the figures look skeptical." Then I mime Joseph and Mary's manger postures of total disbelief.

As a boy, Danny revered Lucille Ball, and *I Love Lucy* was his daily half-hour sanctuary. When Lucy was hospitalized in 1989, Danny shared his genuine concern with Jaffe and me and talked about her so much at the law firm where he temped that on the day she died, his supervisor called and told him not to come in, while assuring him that he'd still be paid. I believe that was the first and only case of gay bereavement leave in history where when your diva dies, you're given time off from work.

Danny especially loved tough, old gravelly voiced Lucille Ball, and he regaled Jaffe and me with stories about her later years. Lucy gave seminars about her career around the country, and she could be brutal during the Q&As. One woman reportedly asked, "Miss Ball, could I come up onstage and give you a big hug?"

"Absolutely not! Next question."

Danny also recalled some young sitcom star was in the audience and kept interjecting her own performance anecdotes during Lucy's seminar. Finally Lucy snapped, "Look, I've seen your show, you're not that funny. Sit down! You might learn something."

These phrases became the first of many "Dannyisms" that became a private Funny Gay Male language. While we watched unfunny, aggressively annoying comics perform, Jaffe would whisper, "Sit down! You might learn something," and I'd crack up. When someone suggested doing something we were vehemently opposed to—supporting Republicans, for instance—we replaced "No" with "Absolutely not! Next question."

Danny also told us about a woman from Queens who became angry with him after she said, "I got the call," and Danny logically asked what the call was about. The woman snapped, "My Archie died!" Soon "I got the call" became our synonym for death, and after the loss of my father, Danny's mother, and Jaffe's father, one of us invariably used the phrase.

In 1991, we became the first out stand-ups to appear on national television on *The Joan Rivers Show*. Before the taping, Joan turned to us and said, "All right, fellas: give me a few serious answers, then Funny, Funny, Funny!" This became a performing mantra that Danny often said to us in Joan's voice before shows to calm our jitters. Danny did a brilliant impression of Joan in his act and after my sister's suicide, he called and left me a serious condolence message followed by Joan referencing her husband's suicide, "Edgar, Edgar, why? WHY?!" Danny added, "Mrs. Smith, that's so wrong. But I think you'll get it." Danny made me laugh at a time when I never thought I'd laugh again.

At the time we did Joan's show, I made most of my income from stand-up, but still cater-waitered to pay my rent. Two months after our taping, a caterer asked if I was available to work Christmas Day. I had just purchased a Mac Classic computer and wanted to buy Microsoft Word. Since working holidays meant double pay, I agreed. "Before you say yes," the caterer warned, "the party's at Joan Rivers's house." We discussed the possible embarrassment at being recognized, but I decided to forgo wearing my usual contact lenses in favor of my glasses, delusionally thinking my Clark Kent "disguise" would work.

Before the party began at Joan's palatial Fifth Avenue condo, which was part of a converted 1903 mansion, she gave the staff a short pep talk. I was relieved when she didn't seem to recognize me.

Later, as I passed a tray of champagne, a guest asked me, "Hey, weren't you on Joan's show?" I nodded yes. "Does Joan know?" I shook my head no. A half hour later, while serving hors d'oeuvres in the library, I felt a hand on my elbow. "Excuse me, everyone!" Joan shouted to the entire room. Conversation stopped. "This is a wonderful comedian. He was a guest on my show!" Joan then said in a low voice, "Isn't this horrifying?" which made me laugh. "Don't let it bother you. You're just starting out. One time, I did a show with Jack Lemmon; then two weeks later I waited on him."

Her gentle mocking reinforced my belief that making a joke in a difficult situation can be an extraordinary act of kindness.

Danny, Jaffe, and I did go through a period where, when one of us was missing, the other two talked about him. I was an angry shrew about the always-late Danny and Jaffe when we traveled, and we performed all over the country, plus Canada and Australia. When we flyered the beaches in Provincetown, Jaffe thought nothing of plopping down on a fan's blanket, leaving Danny and me to cover the rest of the beach, which pissed us off.

But we grew to accept each other's personal foibles, since our friendship had been tested by numerous professional ordeals. There was a manager who booked us for five grand but paid us three. (To get out of our contract with the scumbag, we had to pay him three grand.) We also had to contend with a continually drunken publicist whose press contacts seemed limited to wine magazines. The only benefit of these ordeals was laughing at Danny's truly obscene, half-hour-long monologues about the manager and his dead-on impression of the tipsy publicist.

In each city, we'd rent a car on our day off and take field trips during which we discovered that all three of us liked to smoke a joint, crack jokes, and appreciate nature. Danny and Jaffe were fellow Nature Boys. I saw my first redwoods with them at Muir Woods. In fact, as Danny lit his pot pipe, he joked about starting a fire destroying all the redwoods. We saw a meteor shower at the beach in Provincetown. I saw my first bald eagle with them on Whidbey Island in Washington. On the ferry to the island, we saw porpoises. One time we performed at Highways for two weeks; every day we would drive to Malibu Creek State Park. It was the perfect park for stand-ups since most of the land was donated by Bob Hope. I remember writing jokes under California oaks while my binoculars hung about my neck—in case I saw or heard an interesting bird.

On that trip, I enjoyed my first earthquake—the Northridge quake. After the first violent tremor, Danny cracked from his bedroom that an overweight actress we all knew must have fallen out of her bed. We laughed until the equally violent aftershock scared the shit out of us.

Yes, fat jokes are wrong, but anyone who knows comedians quickly learns that professional boundaries are not the same as our personal boundaries. I would never refer to any woman as a bitch or fat onstage, but I stood in an airport with a sign saying BITCH because my audience was another comedian. It was wrong, but in context, I knew Judy would laugh.

One of our field trips was to the Franklin Roosevelt estate along the Hudson River in Hyde Park. We were on a guided tour of the main house, and Roosevelt's wheelchair was displayed. We stood in the back of the group and Danny said, "Oh, Eleanor, you wouldn't treat me this way if I wasn't in this wheelchair." Then switching to Bette Davis's voice in Baby Jane, he sneered. "But ya-cha in that wheelchair! But, ya-cha!" It was an example of perfect timing and the three of us became so hysterical we had to quit the tour.

When I met Steve Moore, the first comedian to do jokes about being HIV positive, he mentioned being ten years older than me, and I cracked that he had "Model T cells." Our friendship was confirmed by his almost spitting out his orange juice.

AIDS and AIDS benefits were an unfunny, ever-present part of the Funny Gay Males' careers. Several times after shows, guys told us, "I just found out I was HIV positive today, and I didn't think I could laugh, but I did." One night at the Duplex, a gaunt young man and his mother came to the show. He was in his early to midtwenties and used a cane. The young man laughed loudly and repeatedly, but his mother was inconsolable. Afterward, she told us that he had really wanted her to see our show, and she thanked us—although her pain was palpable. It wouldn't be the last time real life entered a comedy club.

The most harrowing show I ever worked was Frank Maya's last performance at Caroline's, a comedy club on Broadway, in 1995. It was a benefit with an all-gay-and-lesbian lineup. Jaffe and Danny were there, and I was asked to emcee. Frank had always been muscular, but his sunken cheeks told me he was sick. It was a moment that happened repeatedly in the eighties and nineties, but the social convention was to behave like nothing was wrong. We were all members of a gay men's chorus whistling in the dark. There was also a manic gleam in his eyes

I'd never seen before. Frank opened his set by declaring, "This is my farewell to comedy."

I'd first met Frank at one of our East Village shows. He was a well-known performance artist who talked to us about coming out in his work, and a short time later he did. (It still seems unbelievable that there was a time in New York when shoving yams in your cooch onstage was permissible, but admitting you were gay was going too far.)

Frank was a pro and had a classic bit about how as a New Yorker he was envious of Anne Frank's hiding place in Amsterdam: "It had a skylight . . ." But that night Frank rambled, and the audience wasn't laughing. Comedy slang for bombing is "dying," and the term had become literal. One asshole shouted, "Get off!" as Frank's fifteen-minute set stretched to over a half hour. The comedians in the room knew he should wrap it up, but there was none of the usual whispered griping that he had gone over his allotted time, a comedy faux pas that is inexcusably rude to the other comedians on the bill. Everyone in the room was transfixed by the stand-up tragedy. For the comedians watching, he was also a piercing reminder that just because you're funny, it doesn't guarantee that you'll be happy. Finally, the manager of the club suggested I stand near the stage and signal to Frank that his time was up. In comedy clubs, there's a small red light that goes on when your time is up, and until that moment I had never considered it to be a metaphor for death. Frank saw me and asked from the stage, "Bob, should I get off?" I nodded my head. It was an agonizingly sad moment and, to this day, I regret not shouting, "NO!" Within a short time, Frank was dead.

One night, a major talent manager had seen me kill. Afterward, he took me aside and said, "You're funny, but why do you have to do the gay stuff? Why can't you just be 'Bob Smith from Buffalo'?" I replied, "Because I'm not ashamed of being gay, but I am embarrassed about being from Buffalo." (That was a joke because I'm actually a booster of my hometown.) The manager added, "They're never going to have anyone gay on *The Tonight Show*."

I immediately knew he was an idiot. There was no proof then that I was ever going to succeed on a big level, but I had worked around New York for over two years, and straight audiences liked my comedy. My first paying gig in New York had been for a Conservative synagogue's singles night. The rabbi had told me how much he enjoyed my set. Of course, I didn't know then that in 1994 I would become the first out gay stand-up on *The Tonight Show*.

As Funny Gay Males' reputation spread, we worked all around New York. At Dixon Place with the fledging Blue Man Group, back when Dixon Place was in an apartment, I suggested onstage that Funny Gay Males should be called Blow Men Group. At La MaMa, we met the legendary Ellen Stewart. We also did numerous benefits at places like the Rainbow Room at Rockefeller Center, hosted by people like Harvey Fierstein—who is as charming and friendly offstage as on. I also worked solo, including one night at the Pyramid Club, where the stage was made up to look like a vagina, and I passed through the birth canal at 1:00 a.m. to do my set.

I knew Judy Gold from Comedy U, but we really became friends when she came to see Funny Gay Males perform in Provincetown. The next day we went to the beach, and Judy and I bonded comedically when the two of us spent several hours loudly repeating variations of the phrase "I make the muffins," in the most annoyingly nasal voices we could create. Judy and her partner, Sharon, were staying at a guesthouse owned by a wealthy gay guy whose penniless partner constantly claimed in his nasal voice that he put the Breakfast in their B&B because he made the lousy muffins (from a mix).

We mined every possible comic twist on "I make the muffins," mimicking his whiny honking endlessly: "I make the sand"; "I make the lesbians"; "I missed the Kadima ball." It was an experience that was enjoyable for comedians but excruciating for anyone else. Finally, Sharon screamed, "Will you two shut the fuck up about the fucking muffins!" People we didn't know on a nearby blanket applauded when they heard her, which only made Judy and me burst out laughing at our own obnoxiousness.

The week after Judy and Sharon left Ptown, I received a call from Sharon telling me Judy's father had died unexpectedly. I immediately called Judy to offer my condolences. She was understandably teary until she angrily mentioned that she had received a "condolence" call from a comedian acquaintance of ours, Jim David, a gay man who is one of what I call the Johnny-Come-Out-Latelys, as he came out onstage in 2000, long after the moment of courage had past. He had brazenly asked Sharon, "Has Judy had to cancel any gigs for the funeral? Because I'd be happy to fill in."

This became a reflexive joke Judy and I still share. Anytime a famous movie star or celebrity died, one of us would immediately call or e-mail, "You know Jim's calling his widow." In fact, when I told Judy that I was diagnosed with ALS, she immediately said this comic would soon call to say how sorry he was and ask if I had any gigs I needed to cancel. Part of my pleasure by then was how with every new twist on that joke, we celebrated our long friendship.

When Judy gave birth to her son Ben in 2001, I was living in LA, and she left a message so suffused with radiant happiness that I didn't erase it for months. A week later she invited me to visit. "If you don't fucking come, I'll fucking kill you!" It was right after 9/11, and Judy was working at Rockefeller Center as a producer on *The Rosie O'Donnell Show*. I visited the same week an NBC News worker tested positive for anthrax and they closed several floors of the building. The following week, Judy was returning to work and she asked if she should be worried. Her question wasn't a joke, and I could see she was anxious.

A few hours later her neighbor knocked on the door and handed me Judy's mail. Judy was changing Ben, and I shouted, "Margery brought the mail. There's an envelope with white powder in it."

Without missing a beat, Judy shouted, "Would you mind opening it?"

"No problem," I replied.

We've been through terrorist attacks, the deaths of our fathers, breakups for both of us, a suicide, and the loss of beloved pets. Judy once called and told me her cat had cancer, and my response was "Was she a smoker?" She laughed and then called me an asshole. She liked my joke so much that she repeated it to all our friends. It would be inappropriate to make such a comment to anyone else, but comedians are artists who intimately face pain in their work. We try out jokes that bomb and know immediately that we've failed.

One thing I admire about Judy is that I've never seen her give a lousy performance. She gives it her all, no matter how bad the audience seems. Emulating her perseverance is how I got my HBO special. In 1993, Madonna's production company flew Funny Gay Males to LA to audition for an HBO gay-and-lesbian comedy special.

The audition was at Igby's, a shabby comedy club, on a rainy Tuesday night. The room was nearly empty, with fifteen customers and a row of HBO big shots sitting in the back. By then, we were friends with several wonderful gay and lesbian comics who weren't part of the lineup, but some of the worst comics I'd ever seen auditioning were there. Several of them had no gay material, clearly they weren't out yet, but they apparently would come out for HBO. One guy did hacky airport jokes that caused Danny, Jaffe, and me to wince during his set. I watched in horror as every comic bombed—including, unfortunately, Danny and Jaffe. For big shows, I always planned my set order in advance, but watching this dreadful train wreck inspired me to open with a different joke and basically wing it. I was incredibly nervous, but from my first joke I got huge laughs and kept making the audience roar. After my set, Danny and Jaffe were incredulous. "Where the fuck did that come from?" Jaffe asked.

I had no idea, but I was thirty-five, had been working as an out comic for seven years, and was impatient for some sign of mainstream success. I had also worked diligently on my act over the past three years in Provincetown, adding signature bits such as declaring why the Catholic Church shouldn't be homophobic: "They should give us credit. We started the Renaissance. It was probably two gay men talking during a party: 'Wouldn't it be fun to sell paintings of hot, muscular, naked guys to churches?' 'Oh, that would be a hoot!'"

After the show, Chris Albrecht, the head of HBO, came over to say how much he enjoyed my set while pointedly ignoring everyone else.

The next day, I got a phone call saying HBO didn't want to do a group show, but they did want to give me my own half-hour special. Then, they gave a lesbian comedian—Suzanne Westenhoefer, a good friend of mine—her own special.

Our HBO specials were favorably reviewed by the television critic of the *New York Times*. It was strange and gratifying to see my name in the paper I'd been reading every day for almost ten years.

After my move to Los Angeles in 1996, Eddie Sarfaty assumed my spot in Funny Gay Males with my blessing. Eddie's ten years younger than the rest of us, muscular, and handsome, and I joked with Danny and Jaffe that people would see the Funny Gay Males poster and say, "The other two have aged horribly, but Bob looks great!"

All four of us eventually performed together, and Eddie became part of our brotherhood. We bonded with him because he's smart and funny, but also because he's an unhappy hunk, prone to depression, and so possesses a great heart and a genuine sense of empathy for others, qualities often lacking in more self-contented hotties.

I also fondly remember a party where a gay Republican defended George W. Bush in front of Danny, Jaffe, Eddie, and me, days after the House Republicans voted to drill in the Arctic National Wildlife Refuge.

I was furious. "You're gay and support Republicans?" I asked.

"Yes," he said. "They're in favor of small government."

"And in favor of big corporations," I said. "Like oil companies that want to drill in wildlife refuges."

"That's free enterprise," he said.

"No, it isn't," I said. "It's greed."

"They're against protecting the environment," Jaffe said.

"It's a refuge!" said Danny. "Not a national refinery."

"And they deny global warming!" said Jaffe.

"People who deny global warming should be fed to polar bears," I said.

"Every time a Republican opens his mouth, he farts!" said Danny.

"And they hate gay people," said Jaffe. "You're like a Jew inviting Hitler to his Bar Mitzvah."

"It's okay to be a bottom in bed," said Eddie, "not in a voting booth."

The host came running out of the kitchen shouting "No politics!" because the four of us had ganged up on the Republican. It's the only time in my life when I've been proud to be a horrible guest.

In 2005, I decided to move back to New York and became Eddie's roommate in his two-bedroom apartment. My return to New York as a stand-up after nine years away was a revelation. There were queer comedy shows all over Manhattan and dozens of gay and lesbian comics. I loved being back in New York, and also fell in love with someone I'd known for twenty years, a sexy writer named Michael Zam, an old friend of Jaffe's. Michael eventually introduced me to the other crazy love of our lives, our dog Bozzie.

New York also seemed happy to have me back. I was thrilled when *Backstage* magazine awarded me their best comedian of the year award in 2006. I also auditioned for the reality show *Last Comic Standing* and made the cut. But I had foolishly stopped dyeing my hair—I went gray in my early thirties—and was eliminated before the show taped, I'm sure due to my looking forty-nine when their prized demographic was eighteen to forty-eight.

One of my proudest moments being back in New York was after Proposition 8 passed in California. The vote to deny marriage equality was heavily backed by the Mormon Church. I was furious that this church had the gall to claim the marriage between two consenting gay or lesbian adults was immoral. Judy called me up and said a demonstration was going to be held in front of the Mormon Temple at 66th and Columbus. She really wanted to go since her two sons, Henry and Ben, were old enough to understand that this bigotry was directed against their family. Eddie and I made signs for Ben and Henry to carry. We all marched, and seven-year-old Ben carried the sign with my joke, "My Two Moms Can Beat Up Your 14 Wives!"

The next day on *The View*, Whoopi Goldberg quoted my joke, and *Salon* magazine also mentioned it. Ben giggled as he marched, and I felt a sense of solidarity with Eddie and Judy, knowing we all understood that sometimes a breezy joke conceals furious contempt.

I was working on my Alaska novel at my desk in Eddie's apartment in May 2006 when Eddie noticed a muscle twitching on the back of my left arm. It turned out to be an early symptom of my ALS. The twitching didn't go away, and I began a long series of medical tests.

That autumn, after I performed for the Human Rights Campaign in Boston, I received a phone call from my agent. She first told me she heard the show went well, then she asked, "Did you drink before the show? Because they said you sounded drunk."

I was horrified and assured her that I never drank or smoked a joint before any performance. Stand-up requires my complete focus and has always been too important to me. My slurring was due to the ALS. I hadn't noticed any problems with my voice, but other people obviously had. I began to start my sets by explaining I wasn't drunk but had a neurological problem.

My explanation worked for a long time, but I have the bulbar variant of ALS that first preys upon the muscles of the tongue and throat. I could still do stand-up and even appeared in 2009 on a Canadian gay comedy special, broadcast from the Winnipeg Comedy Festival. I killed but have never watched that performance. It would be too painful to hear my jokes delivered sloppily.

It was fittingly in a small East Village comedy club in 2010 that I decided to stop performing. There were only ten people in the audience, but I had lost my fear of small audiences back when I auditioned for HBO.

I hadn't performed for several months and immediately noticed how difficult it was to pronounce my jokes, lines I'd done hundreds of times. Jokes that always killed were garnering looks of incomprehension. I apologized and repeated a few lines again. Something I'd never had to do before. After the show, I apologized to the host, who graciously said there was nothing to apologize for. I was in a state of shock.

I had always thought I would perform stand-up for my entire life. When Funny Gay Males performed in Montreal at the Just for Laughs comedy festival, one of the headliners was Milton Berle. He was eighty-three and had made thousands of people laugh, including us. We had followed Milton as we went through Canadian customs and overheard him cracking a joke about the cigar dangling from his lips. "It's a Lawrence Welk cigar," he said. "A piece of shit surrounded by a band."

I envisioned myself cracking jokes at his age.

Of course, the one benefit of having ALS is that whenever my comedian friends vent about their problems—unemployment, relationships, possible eviction from their apartments—I can always trump them by saying "three to five years," which is the Google life span of people with ALS. Now when they discuss their problems, they always jokingly preface them with "I know I don't have ALS, but . . ."

I am proud to have achieved the two biggest goals of all stand-ups: appearing on *The Tonight Show* and having my own HBO special. I also don't feel I've given up comedy since I can still write novels and essays. But it takes so long to become a good stand-up that giving it up was deeply painful; it's even more agonizing when I watch comedians perform who aren't nearly as funny as I am. I'm also incredibly proud of

Funny Gay Males. We had the guts to be out when even Judy was afraid of coming out.

We performed at the first-ever gay and lesbian inaugural ball at President Clinton's inauguration in 1993, along with Kate Clinton and Suzanne Westenhoefer. That year, we also performed at the LGBT March on Washington in front of half a million people. I wrote a new joke for the event: "I think we should have a gay agenda. It would be limited to two things: Number One—Full civil rights. Number Two—We want our national anthem to have a twenty-five-minute dance version." It got the biggest laugh and most thunderous applause of my career. I'm also proud that on Ellen DeGeneres's historic coming-out episode, someone on the show gave a nod to Funny Gay Males by featuring the immediately recognizable purple-and-yellow cover of our book *Growing Up Gay* in a bookstore scene.

My only regret in my stand-up career is that I wish Funny Gay Males hadn't just mimicked the toughness of old showbiz pros like Lucille Ball and Lauren Bacall and had, instead, become as indomitable as they were.

In the midnineties, we were offered the chance to do a six-week Off Broadway run of Funny Gay Males by the prestigious Atlantic Theater Company.

We were eager to move beyond our loyal LGBT audience, but our manager at the time insisted we should turn down their offer and let him raise the money to produce us Off Broadway. He clearly implied he would be deeply hurt if we accepted the Atlantic's offer. (Performers quickly learn that agents and managers have touchier egos than almost any entertainers.) Why we had to be nice guys and didn't stand up for ourselves mystifies me still.

Well, we were nice guys, but we lacked Lucille's balls. Show business produces tough cookies because performers have to make every mistake to learn anything. I know now that we made a colossal error, but it did teach me an invaluable lesson.

For the past ten years, the Angel of Death has become my stalker, following me around from gig to gig, scaring my friends, showing up at my apartment to pester me.

"Mr. Smith, I'm a big fan and wondered if I could hug the life out of you?"

"Absolutely not! Next question."

WWJD

What Would Jackie Do?

Ralph Waldo Emerson wrote the most sensible thing anyone has ever said about religion: "The foregoing generations beheld God and nature face to face; we, through their eyes. Why should not we also enjoy an original relation to the universe?" Unfortunately in our time, Emerson's rhetorical question is frequently regarded as religious intolerance. It's permissible to talk about God in general terms, but offensive to specifically question someone's religious beliefs, no matter how ridiculous they are.

I now was blessed with a free pass to discuss all religions and beliefs after I was forced to confront the fact that my relation to the universe might expire. I had been unaware that my healthy life was a miracle until the day I was diagnosed with ALS. My doctor was understandably uncomfortable giving out his grim diagnosis, and to fill in my silence after his announcement he said nervously, "It's a really rare disease." I responded with "So it's like winning the disease lottery?" A small part of me was surprised that I'd react with a joke, but most of me understood that my being funny was as intrinsic to my identity as my thick hair, lanky stature, and slowly dying motor neurons. The doctor didn't laugh, but his lips moved quickly to cover his inadvertent smile.

When the afterlife moves from an afterthought to a pressing matter, you feel free to take a Judgment Day on your life and all faiths. The obvious thing I first pondered is that there would probably be no religions at all if people didn't die. The purpose of every religion is to tell a comforting bedtime story about our impending dirt nap. But I'm a writer and have found the narrative failure of almost every Good Book is also the failure of every bad novel, movie, or television show; they require the suspension of your intelligence before you're able to suspend your sense of disbelief.

That afternoon, I investigated my illness by googling "ALS/Lou Gehrig's disease" and discovered it was a synonym for "hopeless." But I didn't feel hopeless.

Hope is another aspect of human consciousness that can probably be explained scientifically as neurons high-fiving each other, but science is still struggling to explain how life was created. The reason we need art is that science will always be inadequate at explaining how life is experienced. Don't get me wrong. I'm not an antiscience dolt who refuses to believe in evolution, due to my observation that every right-wing bigoted belief is fixed and unchanging. Or a moron who believes climate change isn't manmade; it's God's way of browning sinners before they're slow-cooked in hell. But I will chalk up one for the faithful as science hasn't yet adequately explained the profound impact love and hope have in our lives.

One of the insights my illness has granted to me is that most of the suffering in our lives can be alleviated more quickly by talking to our friends and family than by praying to God. (I'm sure believers would say God is answering my prayers through people, but you can't have it both ways: either we have free will or we're marionettes controlled by the puppet master in the sky.) Since my diagnosis, much of my stress has come from the numerous, unnecessary human-caused problems dealing with our corporate health care system, which seems designed as a form of euthanasia, since you'd rather die than deal with its pernicious complexities. What's made it bearable is that friends and even a stranger (now a friend) helped me navigate the merciless paperwork.

I've been dealing with my ALS for ten years, and I can honestly say that for the most part my life's been very happy. First of all, I'm mental—certifiably optimistic—and I've spent my life believing I can do almost anything: move to New York, become a successful stand-up comic, write books, snag more than one handsome boyfriend. So surviving a devastating incurable disease seems like another daunting challenge that I have to overcome. I'm uneasy about my health, but I was also anxious about all those other hurdles.

My partner, Michael, has been heroically supportive. Part of his support has been that he can still get really angry with me when I disappoint him: for example, if I don't clean up my papers that I promised to clear off the dining room table last Friday. He'll still treat me like a living boyfriend and not a dying patient. My two brothers have been so generous toward me that I actually forgive them for voting for George W. Bush twice! (Even Jesus would find that tough to forgive.)

All of my friends have been amazingly helpful. They've offered to assist me when I need help, and they also treat me the same: mocking me when the occasion arises. (I'm a funny guy, but I'm starting to think my real talent is in making friends.)

A group of friends I've become especially close to are my New York drinking, talking, writing, and laughing buddies, Patrick Ryan, David McConnell, Don Weise, Michael Carroll, and Chris Shirley. We're all writers or editors, and every Monday night for the past five years we've had a boys' night out at Barracuda, a neighborhood gay bar in Chelsea. Chris's former partner Chuck dubbed us A.S.S.: The Authors Secret Society, a moniker we eagerly adopted. While having cocktails, we enjoy discussing books, boys in general, boyfriends in particular, and then head out to dinner at one of the five restaurants we can all agree on.

I've only known these guys for a short time, but our rapport was instant, mutual, and easy as all good friendships are. We all write about different aspects of the same subject, gay men, in Alaska, Florida, Memphis, or in journalism school and pirate ships, and we have different styles—from high literary to my jokey vernacular—but among the common bonds we share is our seriousness about writing and our levity about almost everything else.

I was diagnosed on a Monday and that night decided to tell the guys. I considered withholding the information, but they had known for months that I'd been undergoing neurological testing for muscle spasms in my arms and slurring problems with my speech. Not telling them on that day would have been like trying to remain nonchalant while a fox hidden under your sweater gnaws on your intestines. I'm always hesitant to tell my news since it's so overpoweringly bad that I'm afraid reminding people how harsh life can be will sink them for weeks. But these guys are well read, and I decided if they could survive the agony of reading Henry James's *The Ambassadors*, they could handle my illness.

They all reacted with teary-eyed empathy and offered to help in any way they could. I felt better immediately after sharing my news with them.

When I told my news to Patrick, he reminded me his partner, Fred Blair, was an acupuncturist and suggested I see him for treatment. Fred is a tall, strawberry blond, telephone pole of a gay man in his forties. We'd met socially and I had immediately liked him since he is smart and funny. (Those two qualifications for friendship are what I look for on everyone's resume.) I didn't know much about acupuncture other than that it had originated in China and involved being poked with needles. But I thought trying something was better than dropping dead limb-by-limb since my doctors at the ALS center didn't offer any ideas on what I could do, beyond sitting back until I needed a wheelchair, and taking Rilutek twice a day. It's the only drug proven to help ALS and adds sixty days to your life expectancy, which is enough time to write a comic essay on religion.

I decided to try acupuncture since I was confident doing anything to prevent my illness would probably add another two months to my life. I called the Blue Lotus Acupuncture Center and made an appointment and then lived my life pretty much as I always did. I woke up and drank two cups of coffee and sat down at my computer to write every day. (Although as a longtime java addict, I've discovered caffeine has never jolted me as effectively as the morning I thought, "Oh, I might be dead soon.") My doctors had also immediately offered to prescribe an antidepressant. (Just one antidepressant sounds inadequate to ALS; it's the kind of illness where you should be munching them like M&Ms.) But I held off on going on antidepressants. I was concerned that the mind-altering substance might affect my writing, and then I'd have to find another antidepressant to fix that. But I also felt pretty happy. My first novel was going to be published that fall and I was booked to perform stand-up on two gay cruises that June. The first trip was to the Galápagos Islands and the second trip, one week later, was a cruise in the Baltic to all the Scandinavian countries and Saint Petersburg. And I was able to bring Michael for free on both of them. I knew I should feel depressed, but I wasn't. Perhaps this was another neurological defect my doctors should investigate. I have no doubt they'd find a cure for that.

A week later, I met Jackie Haught, the senior acupuncturist at Blue Lotus. She's a stocky, sixty-year-old lesbian with short white hair who works in New York City two days a week. The rest of the time she lives and works in Woodstock, New York, with her partner, Phyllis, in a beautiful cozy house surrounded by forest. Jackie's a Tibetan Buddhist, caffeine addict, and can reminisce about an acid trip forty years ago one moment and then talk seriously about the importance of kindness the next. She possesses the rare gift of being able to talk about spirituality without ever making you feel like she's preaching. There's an engaging pragmatism about Jackie's beliefs that keeps them rooted in life, not the afterlife. Jackie believes you must treat people kindly, not to be rewarded with heaven but to be rewarded with a more compassionate earth.

Fred grew up in Louisiana, studied comparative literature at Columbia, and believes a universal intelligence animates the cosmos. He's a genial, easygoing guy who will take a hit off a joint on the weekends but also possesses a keen moral sense of what's right and wrong. Unlike many do-gooders, Fred always gives the amusing impression that he wants to do what's right since it will infuriate the assholes of the world. Be nice to piss off the nasty is actually a sentiment Jesus should have preached about since it's probably a more effective and satisfying way of changing the world for the better.

Neither Jackie nor Fred are saints. They're capable of rolling their eyes at clients who become grumpy filling out the long Blue Lotus patient questionnaire, but I've also observed the grouchiest patients always leave converted to pleasant as if their habitual meanness only needed to be deflated with the stab of a needle.

On my first visit, Jackie and Fred asked a lot of questions about my illness and both had already investigated how acupuncturists in China treat ALS. They also explained to me how acupuncture works. It's about restoring the proper balance of qi (pronounced chi), or life force, in the body and that was enough of a metaphor for me to imagine my body as a household appliance with faulty wiring. I was broken but could be fixed. Jackie and Fred radiated the authority and skill in their field that I can only compare to my knowledge of stand-up comedy. A great stand-up owns the stage, and Jackie and Fred own their examination rooms. I've also discovered over the past three years that we are kindred spirits: Jackie and Fred both have great senses of humor, and yet they're also dedicated and serious about their work.

I immediately felt better after my first treatment. I firmly believe acupuncture works but understand some people might attribute that my relief is due to a placebo effect. So what? All art and literature have a placebo effect on humanity and only an idiot would argue the results from them haven't been proven to be beneficial. When doctors profess skepticism to alternative treatments, I always think you should remember that the mind does affect the body. There's scientific proof of that every time a man gets a boner.

Part of my treatment has been being part of a community where people are more concerned with healthcare than wealthcare. Jackie and Fred work with a group of men and women, straight and gay, who, in exchange for acupuncture treatments, offer massage, bookkeeping, or—as I did before I lost my voice—fill in at the front desk one day a week. Jackie and Fred's example of charity will never make them rich, but they've made me believe the simplest definition of a great life is thinking that anyone who has known you has been lucky.

Everyone who knows Jackie and Fred feels like they've won the lottery.

It seems hard to know how to live a good life, but once the Angel of Death's sickle touches your throat I can promise much of your confusion will clear up. Life really isn't that complicated. First, the golden rule of all religions is love thy neighbor as thyself, which surprisingly is first mentioned in the book of Leviticus. Antigay bigots never quote that injunction from their Handbook of Hatred since it also evidently gives God's stamp of approval to all forms of mutual masturbation.

It's also easy to figure out what we need to do to make the earth more heavenly. First, always err on the side of compassion and kindness. We have millions of self-professed Christians in this country whining that they shouldn't pay taxes for healthcare or food stamps for their neighbors or education for their neighbor's children. Why? Because these loving Christians with hearts like tight fists worry some of their almighty dollars might be wasted. If Jesus returns, there's no doubt the first thing he'll do is throw these moneychangers out of the voting booth.

I'm not a believer in any faith, but I'm not ready to declare that I'm an atheist either. I have serious doubts as to the existence of the God (or gods) worshipped by various religions, but I'm also a connoisseur of the cosmic. Following Emerson's dictum, I've eyed the universe and have witnessed and experienced things that I don't believe can be explained by science. In fact, scientific explanations often sound as plausible as Genesis.

For example, the physicist Stephen Hawking explains the creation of the universe from nothingness by the force of gravity while other people attribute it to God. Both arguments aren't particularly convincing. They both explain the Big Bang with words that begin with a *g* and neither argument is ever going to be proved conclusively. But both stories are cosmic. (Stephen acknowledges the Divine might be involved.) The universe was created from nothing and that fact should give pause to every thoughtful person. So following my own rule that it's okay to be skeptical, but it's wrong to be cynical, I'm open to the idea of God, but these are my Ten Deal Breakers for a religion:

1. I shall not believe in a God who's meaner than I am.
2. I shall not believe in any religion that claims God has a dress code.
3. I shall not believe in any religion where any form of consensual sex is a sin.
4. I shall not believe in any religion where men and women aren't equal.
5. I shall not believe in any religion that doesn't accept that its creation myth is a metaphor.
6. I shall not believe in any religion that places more emphasis on the afterlife than life.
7. I shall not believe in any religion that refuses to admit that dull and unquestioning preaching about your beliefs is the most unoriginal of sins.
8. I shall not believe in any religion that doesn't honor the earth and animals.

9. I shall not believe in any religion that excuses my being a greedy, selfish asshole for my entire life if I repent on my deathbed.
10. I shall not believe in a God without a sense of humor.

I was raised Roman Catholic. In the first grade, in preparation for my first communion, I started attending religious instruction classes, where I was first exposed to the doctrines of Christianity. Our teacher was Sister Annette, a wizened, ancient nun with rimless eyeglasses who looked old enough to have been third in line when original sin was first handed out. She enthusiastically told the story of Adam and Eve as if she was reading a children's book where Jack and Jill went up the hill and ate God's fruit, instead of their vegetables, and then came down the hill among the fallen.

"You're all sinners and you were born sinners!" she trilled at the close of her tale.

Why is this story considered appropriate for first-graders? The doctrine of original sin is a form of child abuse: a heavenly father telling us we're inherently evil—sinners from birth. If a mortal father did that to his children, it would be considered psychological abuse and his children would be placed in foster care. Every sensible person would jettison the idea of original sin if they thought of the concept in a whiny teenage girl's voice: "Jesus Christ! Excuse me for living!"

As a writer, I admire the engrossing story of Adam and Eve. It's a love story with betrayal, nakedness, a talking snake, and God's food issues. The Almighty forbids Adam and Eve to eat his apple of knowledge and when they do, God goes bananas and mandates they and their progeny's last suppers will be sucking on the bitter lemon of death.

The one inspiring element of the story of Adam and Eve is that, according to the Bible, which fundamentalist Christians believe to be entirely true, God created Adam and then he created Eve out of one of Adam's ribs. In other words, God performed the first sex change operation. Every time a man lies with a woman, he's actually hooking up with a man's rib, which means, according to the Bible, there is no such thing as heterosexuality.

Everyone's gay.

Therefore, according to the Bible, Adam and Eve really *are* Adam and Steve.

Hey, it's in the Bible.

Even as a kid, I had problems with the idea of our father who art in heaven. He's in the other room watching over us and our belief in him must serve as our night-light. Only it turns out if we're scared and scream for help, he'll ignore us. My father and mother always comforted me when I hurt myself, while we're told God loves us, but his ways are mysterious and we can't depend on him. When you consider that parent-child scenario as a basis for a religion it sounds like mankind's original sin was gullibility.

The heavenly father or heavenly mother metaphor really fell apart for me after I became a donor to a lesbian couple and had a son and a daughter. First of all, I would never want to create children with abilities inferior to mine. In fact, I hope they'll surpass me. So when I hear God created man in his own image but skipped giving us omniscience and immortality, it makes God the father sound like he deliberately set out to have mentally retarded, terminally ill children, which is inconceivable to any real dad.

And what loving parent threatens his children with eternal punishment? Love me or I'll torch you sounds like the textbook definition of an unhealthy relationship, a relationship any sane psychologist would recommend ending. If God really wanted us to have true freewill he would have given us his omnipotent abilities to go off and create our own universe after we decided our relationship with him wasn't working. Instead God offers love by coercion where the choice is him or burning.

Wait, we're being asked to love a God who burns people alive for eternity?

If there's one ecumenical history lesson everyone agrees upon, it's that people who burn people are evil. No one defends witch roasts or Nazi crematoriums—so a God who burns people for any reason is evil. Yes, all religions that reek of brimstone stink to high heaven.

(I'm not counting Hitler or the rest of the Nazis. They should burn eternally.)

Sister Annette gave us the Roman Catholic version of sexual education when she briefly discussed Jesus's virgin birth. The annunciation is troubling because an angel just delivers the news that Mary is going to carry God's child after the Holy Ghost haunts her vagina. There's no discussion or permission asked because God is a man and most men believe any women carrying his child has received a great honor.

Sister Annette repeatedly reiterated that God killed his only son to show his love for us, just as I assumed she mistreated first-graders to demonstrate her love for them. She also said Jesus was a gift. Let me get this straight: If pagan religions like the Mayans cut the beating heart out of a man to demonstrate their love for their gods, it's barbaric, but if God lets his son be nailed to a cross, it's the equivalent of a cosmic hug? Killing your son to prove your love is like sending an actual bloody heart as a valentine. God created the universe, but he couldn't come up with a more affirming demonstration of love? Christianity's house of God seems like a house of cards that would collapse if one person said to the Almighty, "There's enough chilling horror in the world without killing people to demonstrate your love. Why can't you just send us gift baskets? And it would be nice to hear you say 'I love you' once in a while."

Christians, take it from a gay guy, men who don't communicate are the worst people to be in a relationship with, and God has been giving us the silent treatment for eons.

I didn't remain a Catholic once I learned the Church sat out the Holocaust, covered up the sexual abuse of thousands of children, and then had the gall to declare that homosexuality is "intrinsically evil." (Catholic apologists always mention Pius XII spoke out publicly twice about Nazi atrocities. Yeah, without mentioning the Jews once. Basically, the shortest of Anne Frank's diary entries is longer than anything the pope ever said publicly about the Nazis.) Look, if your pope watched silently as a million Jewish children were slaughtered and then his successors tolerated sexually abusing thousands of kids, I'd say those abominations have ended your moral stature for eternity. It's hard to claim to be advocates of the kingdom of heaven after actively aiding and abetting hell on earth. I'm sure these statements will draw forth accusations of anti-Catholic bias, but those are the facts. If the Roman Catholic Church is the best Christianity can do, then why not just worship Satan since I assume he's also fine with killing and abusing children?

My partner Michael is Jewish and I've come to believe the other monotheistic faiths are cheap knockoffs of the original from my observation of the Jewish holidays—for Rosh Hashanah and Passover you prepare a nice dinner and invite friends over for brisket and serve side dishes where the color green is traif. Roman Catholic hospitality is parsimonious in comparison. All we do is talk about the nice dinner someone had two thousand years ago and then commemorate it by eating little bits of stale bread and maybe having a sip of wine.

The Jewish faith depicts God as a put-upon, perpetually temperamental father or, at best, an unbearable uncle who pinches your cheek as he tells you an unfunny joke. God commanded Abraham to sacrifice his son Isaac, and just as Abraham was about to fulfill his duty, God said, "Just kidding!"

The story of the book of Job is more troubling. It says that God and the devil made a bet about whether Job would remain faithful to God if Satan inflicted horrors upon him and his family. (First of all, isn't God all-knowing? Doesn't he know the outcome of everything? If he does, then what's the point of making Job suffer? Are God and Satan just bored? Their wager makes dogfighting seem almost benign.) Satan sends a wind that causes all of Job's children to be killed and yet Job remains faithful and says the Lord giveth and the Lord taketh away. The book of

Job is unsettling since its obvious message is that no one individual is important to God. Those first-born kids were snuffed to test a theory. Since God knew the outcome ahead of time, the story of Job is as mindlessly vicious and cruel as the unnecessary testing of known ingredients that cosmetics companies do on rabbits and beagles. If the all-knowing God knows everyone's fates, all three monotheistic faiths turn him into a heartless lab technician tallying up the results of painful experiments whose results were never in question.

The Jewish people also claim they have a special covenant with God. It's hard to believe the Jews, of all people, didn't run that contract past a lawyer since the Holocaust alone makes me think they didn't read the fine print. Every year I'm reminded again of the beauty of Jewish traditions due to Michael's family. His sister, Michelle, and her husband, Jeremy, always invite us to their house for Passover and Rosh Hashanah. Jeremy's parents, Sam and Edith, are usually also guests. He's eighty-six and she's eighty-two, and they disprove the myth that you have to become set in your ways when you grow old. They're a delightful, charming couple who always make Michael and me feel welcome. Edith enjoys talking about books and travel with the verve of a twenty-year-old. She also spent her fourteenth birthday in Auschwitz. (I mentioned to Michael, "You do know the most upbeat, non-neurotic person in your family is the Holocaust survivor?" Michael laughed and responded, "Well, wouldn't you be upbeat if you survived the Holocaust?")

At her granddaughter Amanda's Bat Mitzvah, I was moved to tears when Edith stood with her in the Temple. Of course, the performer in me wanted Edith to crow at that moment, "Fuck you, Hitler!" and then sing, "I'm still here!" from Sondheim's *Follies*.

At Rosh Hashanah this year, Edith mentioned to me that she had gone to temple that day and had read in the day's lesson that "God is always just."

"It's upset me all day," she said in her melodic middle-European accent. "God isn't always just. My twin brother was killed. My cousin's baby and my parents. Their deaths weren't just. It's not right and I'm writing my rabbi about it."

I was deeply moved by Edith's thoughtful approach to her religion. It's not a simple leap of faith for her to remain observant, but she also remains true to her experience. She's faced the universe at gunpoint and her faith in her own powers of reasoning made me believe that she would tell God to his face that he's unjust. And I have no doubt that would be a divine moment. I admire that the Jewish faith permits you to have a difference of opinion with our Father who art in heaven and not get kicked out of the family.

Of course some Jewish beliefs are puzzling to this goy. For example, the kosher rule not to mix meat and dairy. But don't cows mix meat and dairy? This sounds like the genesis for the venerable Jewish tradition of the punch line.

The younger sibling of monotheism is Islam, but once I read that Muhammad led wars against neighboring tribes I lost interest in investigating that religion. Surely a prophet of God should be able to resist the temptation of going to war? Jesus and Buddha were peaceniks and I think the standard they set has to be observed by all prophets of God. The other thing I find off-putting about Islam is that they consider dogs to be ritually unclean animals. This may be a personal failing of mine, but my dog, Bozzie, is my friend, and if someone speaks badly of my friends, I want to have nothing to do with them. But my knowledge about Islam is limited and Emerson would never claim I'm having an original relationship with the universe by looking up Islam on Wikipedia. Certainly anyone who's seen Islamic architecture will come away thinking Allah has an equal claim on our spirituality. I've also been appalled by the freely expressed anti-Islamic bigotry spouted in our country. I've traveled to an Islamic nation, Turkey, four times and loved every minute of it—Edith loves Istanbul also—and most of the Muslims I've ever met there were nicer than most of the Christians I hear on radio or see on television. The tragedy of Christians, Jews, and Muslims is they all claim to worship the same King of Kings, but each of them claims to be the favorite daughter of this Lear Above Us and then proceed in turn to behave like Goneril and Regan treated Cordelia.

I believe all good books should be judged on their literary merits. If a religion tells a story that is hateful, prejudiced, or clumsily implausible, even in part, it's not a good book.

The pick and choose morality of religions is also a deal breaker. All three orthodox branches of the monotheistic faiths are officially homo-phobic, sexist, and for most of their history tolerated slavery. In the Bible there are more prohibitions against usury than there are against homosexuality, but banning marriage between bankers is a nonstarter since it would probably hurt the church, mosque, and synagogue fund-raising drives.

I firmly believe all denominations deserve our tolerance, but many of them don't deserve our respect. The Mormons didn't officially con-sider African Americans equal until 1978! Yeah, God suddenly changed his mind about black people after he listened to all the great funk music in the seventies and then he relayed the revelation to his prophet Spencer W. Kimball in Salt Lake City.

The Mormons also lead the campaign against marriage equality for gay couples, but never mention their founder Joseph Smith married a fourteen-year-old when he was thirty-eight. They also omit their second leader, Brigham Young, proved he liked to fuck 'em young when he married a fifteen-year-old when he was forty-two! So Mormons please lecture the gays that marriage is reserved for a man and a woman because you're the experts on the subject with those shining examples of marriage between middle-aged men and middle school kids.

Of course, the Southern Baptists also loudly proclaim the gays are sinners even though their church was formed in 1845 to support slavery. I really want to worship in the Plantation House of God with old slave cabins out back. (They probably called them "slave mangers" to make them sound more Christian.) If an organization is founded for an evil

purpose can any good come of it? Let's see, your church was formed
to support separating children from their parents and auctioning them
off, and yet you now claim to defend families? I know God is old, but
he doesn't have Alzheimer's. He's not going to forget that his supposed
followers, devils with a drawl, allowed children to be whipped and sold
and then each week dropped their blood money in the collection plate,
or that his other followers allowed children to be slaughtered by the Nazis
and molested by priests, or that his other followers married children.
And yet they all claim love between consenting same-sex adults is sinful.

The ancient Greeks would call that hubris. Religious faith is by definition unproven, but many believers possess an overweening arrogance
that allows people to behave despicably due to their smug conviction
they're doing the right thing. For the most part the ancient Greeks told
bedtime stories that made even the most rewarding afterlife sound like a
punishment. The Iliad and Odyssey were the touchstones of ancient
Greek religious and cultural beliefs, and they're probably the only two
examples of Good Books that are actually enjoyable to read. Every edu-
cated Greek was familiar with the works of Homer, and in book II of
the Odyssey, Odysseus visits the land of the dead and meets Achilles.
Achilles died a hero's death, a death the Greeks honored, but he appears
to Odysseus in a dream and tells him that living as a *metic*, basically a
serf enslaved to a tenant farmer, a man with no home, anathema to the
Greeks, would be better than being a dead hero in the afterlife. This is a
chilling message every Greek knew and while it's one of the most beautiful passages in all of literature, it's not exactly comforting about death
and the afterlife.

The Greeks had no fixed canon or bible about their gods, and every
generation was allowed to have an original relationship with their universe and tell their stories anew. The stories of the Greek gods, like the
best stories in our Bible, capture a sophisticated and often dark view of
life and human nature. Demeter caused autumn and winter because she
was depressed about being separated from her daughter, Kore, who had

to spend six months a year as a prisoner of Hades. It requires a nimble and witty culture to make a riveting story about seasonal affective disorder.

One major difference between our one God and a Greek god is they all had sex, except for Athena, who remained a virgin, although she seemed to take out her frustration by being a goddess of war. Zeus and Apollo were bisexual. It's great to have a religion that isn't homophobic plus gods that are hotties.

According to his unflattering portrait in the Old Testament, our God is more into stoning than getting his rocks off. We're told our God is love, but he never gets laid. Uh-oh. That explains a lot. We all know from experience, if someone's not getting any and they're in a position of authority over you, you're fucked. And even worse, our God's watching his creations boink all the time. Which turns our God into the strangest sort of wanker pervert leering at us through the clouds. And does anyone really believe a God who's never had any kind of sex is in any position to judge the sex lives of consenting adults? If a human did that we'd just blame his disapproval on envy.

Of course, the Three Stooges of Monotheism and the dysfunctional family of Mount Olympus aren't the only faiths on earth. There are the Eastern religions of Buddhism and Hinduism. They ask everyone to buckle down and seek enlightenment. It sounds good until I discovered the path to enlightenment is by reincarnation.

Reincarnation is a school system where almost everyone is a slow learner who keeps flunking the final. But is the almost universal rate of failure the fault of the students or the educational system? Is it fair that everyone's memories of their previous lives are wiped clean like a blackboard and we have to start from scratch each time? Reincarnation comes off as an idiotic way to impart wisdom. You have to relearn every life lesson repeatedly as if childhood, adolescence, adulthood, middle age, and old age were flashcards you were too dumb to memorize when you were a priest in ancient Egypt. Not to mention that reincarnation is responsible for the idea of karma and this notion of cosmic justice has been misused to treat other people as "untouchables," one of the most unjust and repellent ideas in history.

Buddhists also believe in rebirth, but it doesn't guarantee your soul will return to be reborn. The Buddhist concept of reincarnation is closer to cosmic recycling where if you lived as a plastic bottle and were good, you might come back as an inflatable pool chair, but if you were bad, you'll come back as a toilet seat. Many of my close friends are Buddhists and I actually appreciate the cosmic ambiguity of their concept of the afterlife. I can live with a mystery, but one of the five tenets of Buddhist belief is that life is suffering.

I don't buy that. Life includes suffering, but for the most part, my life's been fun, even after I was dealt a poker hand with four Angels of Death. I have a hunch that if Buddhists stopped believing life is suffering the world would suddenly be a lot pleasanter for Buddhists and non-Buddhists alike.

Now many people find spiritual inspiration in the natural world. One of my favorite writers and one of Emerson's best friends was Henry David Thoreau, who said, "Heaven is under our feet as well as over our heads." It's a sentiment I concur with as I've definitely felt a cosmic sense of awe when I've witnessed a hundred blue-footed boobies plummet from the sky into the ocean in the Galápagos, seen fifty killer whales rising from the sea in Alaska, walked through redwoods, admired the chilly fire of New England's forests in autumn, or seen a hummingbird courageously sitting on its nest, even though a big plodding birdwatcher was gawking two feet away.

I revere the natural world and believe there are many places on earth where you can feel we never left Eden. Finding God in nature seems initially comforting since, like Thoreau, I also prefer hugging strange trees to strange people.

Many fundamentalist Christians support right-wing nutjobs who oppose protecting the earth. (I never use the word "conservative" because right-wing "conservatives" don't conserve anything.) They're ignoring numerous Bible verses about caring for God's creation. "I now establish my covenant with you and with your descendants after you and with every living creature that was with you—the birds, the livestock, and all the wild animals, all those that came out of the ark with you—every living creature on earth" (Genesis 9:9–10).

That's *every* living creature. I'm not going to allow wolverines to go extinct because selfish greedy men are determined to make the world an office.

Worshiping Nature isn't easy once you realize your reverence for the Grand Canyon also has to include bowing down before smallpox. Nature is not a merciful god, and as Thoreau lay dying of tuberculosis, I bet he would have gladly said, "Fuck Nature! Give me some antibiotics."

Some religions tell stories of such beauty that they express the cosmic. The Yup'ik of Alaska believe everything has a soul: animals, people, rocks. A belief I embrace. When Yup'ik women collected driftwood on the beaches for their fires, they would occasionally overturn a piece in order to make the wood more comfortable and relieve it from sitting in the same position. To me, that belief is cosmic and comic. Showing compassion to a tree limb is a more profound expression of hope than a guy hanging on a cross. If we can learn to be considerate to wood, maybe we won't end up being selfish pricks for our entire lives.

Isn't it time to consider a God who's not our crazy shut-in relative in the attic? Do we need a God who makes us jump through hoops to earn our haloes? Shouldn't we believe that the God who created the cosmos isn't petty and small-minded? And shouldn't we have a religion that's also based upon faith in people like Jackie and Fred? Even if people only answer your prayers 10 percent of the time, that's a track record that beats God's. There's nothing wrong with believing in a loving God, and my emphasis is on a loving God, as many religions still profess a belief in a vindictive God, but Fred and Jackie have made me believe talking to people should be the first thing you should try; if that doesn't work, then pray.

Oh, and if people believe God gave me ALS because I'm gay, or he's sending two middle-aged lesbians to hell for kissing or barbecuing a scared teenage girl for having an abortion, it's the opposite of divine love. It's time to stop tolerating the idea that religions that hurt and kill people aren't evil, out of a sense of misguided politeness. It's time to exercise our right and duty to demonstrate we love our neighbors by fighting against intolerant faiths. Religions that preach hate should die and go to their bigot heaven where the angel's robes are accessorized with Klan hoods. If you insist on believing in a vengeful God, I pray that my loving God will punish your hateful intolerance for eternity by sending you to heaven, where you'll get a pair of angel's wings and then discover you're allergic to feathers.

So what sort of religion would I advocate? My bible would be two paragraphs:

Anton Chekhov wrote, "My holy of holies is the human body, health, intelligence, talent, inspiration, love, and the most absolute freedom imaginable, freedom from violence and lies, no matter what form the latter two take." And Walt Whitman wrote, "This is what you shall do: Love the earth and sun and the animals, despise riches, give alms to every one that asks, stand up for the stupid and crazy, devote your income and labor to others, hate tyrants, argue not concerning God."

It is pointless to argue about God since the only people who claim to have spoken to him are usually certifiably insane. My problem with most religions is they encourage procrastination by holding out the afterlife as the place where all our problems will be solved, rather than pointing out that most human problems can be remedied here on earth. I'm more afraid of dying horribly, being unable to walk, talk, eat, write, or wack off than I am of being dead. And God is not going to prevent me from dying horribly; people will. People will find a cure for my disease and people like Jackie and Fred give me hope.

God has to be Love—any other alternative is universally unacceptable—but many Christians wear bracelets bearing the initials

WWJD: What Would Jesus Do? First of all, Jesus never once mentioned homosexuality and so fundamentalists should follow his example and shut the fuck up. Second, seeking to emulate Jesus is setting yourself up to fail, since you can't get news that you're going to be crucified and vow to rise from the dead three days after you croak.

I have proof of the goodness of people and faith that love and compassion can make even the horrors of a monstrous disease bearable and reveal that heaven on earth is possible. My partner, Michael, proves this to me every day and so does my best friend, Eddie. Jackie is truly the most compassionate, loving person I know. She's changed my life more than God, although I am open to the idea God brought her into my life. I can always figure out how to do the right thing by just asking myself: What Would Jackie Do?

I've had a funny amazing life and get a terminal illness when I'm forty-seven? I have no qualms about asking the God of Love, Who the hell brought me on the early train? I bet Anne Frank and Jesus would back me up. If I'm admitted through the gates of heaven, I expect shirtless Apollo to be waiting. He'll ask me out for a date and then I'll believe in paradise.

At Walden Pond with Henry

John, guess where I am."

"Sitting in front of your laptop, either writing something funny or checking out something filthy."

"Good guess, but no. I'm at Walden Pond. Doesn't it seem hilariously wrong to have good cell reception here?"

"It's hilariously wrong to use your cell phone there. Thoreau would be pissed."

"No, he wouldn't. I'm right outside a replica of his cabin. Henry was a New Yorker. He built a studio apartment in his Central Park. And you know how we New Yorkers love our cell phones."

Walden Pond State Reservation is a characteristic example of how we enjoy nature: 2,680 acres of protected forest enhanced by several acres of parking lots. I continued to chatter with John while walking under the shade of tall trees and admiring the pond where wilderness preservation first dipped a toe in the water, when a man stepped into my path.

"John, I have to go. I'll call you later."

"Bob, I'm trying to savor this grove," said the man. "But it's an insurmountable task due to your ceaseless hubbub. You're aggravating the cicadas."

It felt as if I had chugged a can of adrenaline. Had I dropped dead? The man who scolded me looked exactly like Henry David Thoreau.

And then he introduced himself. "Thoreau here. But call me Henry." Henry's tight-lipped mouth looked like a corral for untamed words. His trimmed dark beard, long nose, lean build, and brown suit give him the air of a schoolmaster, but his memorable blue-gray eyes made me sense he would teach me something that would change my life.

I explained the reason for my call, pointing out that my friend is a fellow Nature Boy, and that he mocked me for using a machine for anything at Walden Pond.

Henry grinned. "I understand. My favorite call of the wild is making a friend laugh."

"I'll put my phone in my car," I said, trying to placate my literary idol.

"You shiftless gadabout. You were just in Concord. You could have walked here." Then he mimicked my flat Buffalo accent, "I'm an environmentalist, but I evolved legs to push gas pedals—not to walk or ride a bicycle."

"Henry, if you hadn't written *Walden*, Americans wouldn't be driving here."

"If I hadn't written *Walden*, the pond would be surrounded by condominiums."

Let's face it. You'll never win a debate with one of your favorite writers, especially if he's dead. Henry is one of my Nature Boys, which means he can hang out with me anytime, in addition to mocking me when the occasion calls for it.

Since my diagnosis of ALS, I feel a particular kinship with Thoreau. He enjoyed walking through the woods while wolf packs of tuberculosis bacteria ripped out his lungs, and I dreamily hike among pine trees while my own body becomes a graveyard of dead-and-buried motor neurons.

"Henry, are you my Angel of Death?"

I explained to him about my you're-gonna-die-agnosis.

"Like I would help that bonehead?" he asked. "I hate Death. He made my life miserable." He reached out and hugged me, giving me a brief whiff of an era before the Age of Deodorant.

Henry said, "A life-threatening illness is like being chopped with an axe. You hope the axe breaks or the woodcutter tires while you still can enjoy being a tree in a forest."

"Or you hope the woodcutter quits chopping to kiss you."

"A woodcutter's kiss is a satisfying hatchet to your heart."

"You sound like the Henry I've read."

"I'm not the author you book-wormed. Since my death, I've observed the extinction of passenger pigeons, Carolina parakeets, and ivory-billed woodpeckers. Birdwatching isn't meant to be an everlasting farewell. Selfish, greedy men are making the world as humdrum as they are. You'll never enjoy seeing a tantivy of wild pigeons."

"I remember reading *Walden* and having to dictionary 'tantivy.' It means swift or rapid."

"Of course, you'd have to look it up. The goddamn pigeons are gone!"

His eyes looked coldly menacing. "I'm not going to permit you or anyone else to witness the extermination of polar bears, rhinoceroses, or tigers. Everyone on earth has to understand: treat Mother Nature like dirt, and she'll bury you."

I had read Thoreau but forgot that the reason he was in favor of civil disobedience was that he was passionate. He was fierce about his love of nature, opposition to slavery, and not having the words chiseled on your tombstone be more fascinating than your life.

Henry smiled. "You're healthy if you feel being alive for a minute is better than dwelling on being in heaven for eternity."

"People waste too much time," I said. "They think clock hands are applauding when they're really giving us the finger."

Henry stopped to admire an old oak tree. "This was probably an acorn when I was here."

Being surrounded by trees never feels claustrophobic, whereas one climate-change-denying Oklahoma senator on television makes the earth feel too crowded. "The trees here are so majestic," I said.

"Yes, they are." His grin autumned into a frown. "It's time to halt the assassination of Mother Nature. We need Birnam Wood to stop these murderers."

"That would be a great name for an environmental activist group: Birnam Wood."

"Bob, you and your friends might have to launch that organization. The earth has a fever, and it might not recover."

"*Macbeth* is one of my favorite Shakespeare plays. It never occurred to me that I loved it because a forest metes out justice to an evil man. I also love Tolkien's *Lord of the Rings* for the same reason."

"I revere the Ents," said Henry. "Sentient walking-and-talking trees that guarded forests and went to war after the evil wizard Saruman cut the ancient trees of Fangorn to use as fuel in his war-making kilns."

"You've read it?"

"Yes. It's only in hell that you can't read. Every book there is burned."

"Unfortunately, the Ents won't rescue my children's planet."

I told Henry about my daughter, Maddie, and my son, Xander.

"My kids love wild animals as much as I do. Xander has a thick illustrated book of mammals, and when he was four, when I pointed to any picture, he could name the animal—from a gnu to a platypus. After a visit to Buffalo's zoo, Xander imitated gorillas for the next month. And when her teacher went around Maddie's class asking each student what animal they'd like to be, there were crates of dogs, cats, and bunnies. Only Maddie said, 'A pygmy marmoset!' My favorite picture of Maddie is of her holding a tiny earthworm in her palm. Her delighted smile seems to say, 'Look at this slimy, precious jewel!'"

"I wish I had kids the way you did. In my time lesbian couples weren't soliciting sperm donors."

"It's a shame you never met and married Emily Dickinson. She was in love with Susan Gilbert. In the nineteenth century, a gay man getting hitched to a lesbian would be having your wedding cake and eating it too."

"I loved Emerson's son Edward. He understood me better than his father."

"Edward loved you, too. His memoir celebrates Thoreau the popcorn maker."

"Popcorn makes people happy, since it's the only food that enjoys being roasted."

Henry's comment made me beam as we arrived at a narrow beach on the pond.

"You've reminded me of the dumbest thing a great writer ever wrote," I said. "After your death, Ralph Waldo Emerson wrote about you, 'I cannot help counting it a fault in him that he had no ambition. Wanting this, instead of engineering for all America, he was the captain of a huckleberry party.' No ambition? Your ambition was to be a great writer, and you achieved it by writing *about* huckleberry parties."

"Emerson was more stern Ralph than gleeful Waldo. He was a great man who couldn't fully enjoy walking in a forest. The trees only made him think of working at his wooden desk."

The beach was crowded with sunbathers. Every body aped a shore-loving animal species from blubbery elephant seal to frisky sea otter to a squawking gull looking for a snack.

"It's gratifying that people still swim here," said Henry. "I swam here with my friend Ellery Channing."

"Ellery said when you laughed it was an operation sufficient to split a pitcher. His comment made me wish you and I were contemporaries."

A red-haired Adonis with a perfectly sculpted torso rose out of the water, and both of us watched him walk to his towel on the beach. He joined his equally alluring girlfriend.

"Nature is beautiful," I said pointedly.

"The birds and the bees are an echo that some body parts are more flighty than others."

"In *Walden*, there's an infatuated portrait of a twenty-eight-year-old, blue-eyed, bushy-haired, woodchuck-eating, French-Canadian woodchopper. Did you swim naked with him?"

"Alek Therien," said Henry. "Now, he was a beautiful man. His hairy chest was my favorite meadow."

"You can't read what you wrote about him and not sense the love and desire—especially the revealing aside about the lovers Achilles and Patroclus. Clearly you would have made room in your bed for some Québecois ooh-la-la. Please tell me you two hooked up?"

"Isn't it obvious? I repeatedly emphasize his animal nature. Every man's cock is a parrot squawking, 'Polly wants him' or 'Polly wants her.'"

"I think both our parrots are pollying for him." I nodded toward an African American hunk in a red Speedo. Henry looked and said, "Squawk!"

"Last summer I came here in the evening with my friends Eddie Sarfaty, Stephen McCauley, and his partner, Sebastian Stuart," I said. "They're all wonderful writers who are kindhearted and wickedly funny."

"It's my favorite oxymoronic phrase."

"Mine too. It was about seven o'clock, and while my pals swam, I stayed onshore with my shirt on; my atrophying muscles make me feel like a vain peacock who's lost his tail."

"We should judge our lovers by comparing them to our relationship with our bodies," said Henry. "Our bodies always disappoint us with flab and wrinkles, and eventually we're married to a murderer. It's an abusive relationship we're all trapped in."

"Tell me about it. It's like I'm dating Jack the Ripper!"

A bright-red male cardinal flew and landed on a shrub to our right. "Cardinals are new additions to the pond," Henry said. "They used to live only in the southeast."

"Bird books claim bird feeders are the cause of their range expansion. I don't buy that."

"They should be the symbol of global warming—a tropical-looking bird breeding in Canada."

"While my friends swam," I continued, "a brown mama mallard— I recognized the species from the female's distinctive iridescent-blue speculum feathers . . ."

"Bob, I know how to identify mallard ducks."

"Of course you would," I said. "Sorry about that."

"I just didn't want you to believe I was duck ignorant. Please continue."

"Her ten ducklings were scampering on this beach. The mama duck kept a sharp eye on her curious offspring who were running near me and also wading into the water like kids playing. The pond is a playground for people and animals."

"Bob, you know me from my books. What made you walk into the wild?"

"I've always been a Nature Boy. The first adult book I owned was a Golden Field Guide for reptiles and amphibians. My fascination with the natural world even withstood watching a garter snake unhinge its jaws and bite the back of my hand. My jaw dropped in astonishment after it left a complete oval of bloody pinpricks. The momentary pain was completely overshadowed by how cool it was to witness a snake's flat bite for the first time."

"When an animal fangs you and draws blood and your heartfelt response is 'Thank you!' you're a Nature Boy."

"Its chomp taught me that fear is a two-way street. A wildly enthusiastic eight-year-old boy is what every garter snake wants to avoid while taking a morning slither through a meadow."

"I wouldn't allow boys to kill snakes on our hikes," said Henry.

"I loved that."

"Well, if you kill snakes because you think they're Satan, you're the one who's evil."

Henry and I slowly strolled down the beach while I blurted out my Nature Boy adventures: bird watching in Central Park, sixteen trips to Alaska, traveling with my partner, Michael Zam, to the Galápagos Islands, and finally admitting that I'm a size queen and love whales and redwoods.

There was a tiny prick on my arm. Looking down, I saw a mosquito lifting off, sporting a beer belly of blood.

I said, "I've been trying to determine why some people fear mosquitoes like vampires, whereas I think of their nibbling me as if I were a walking bag of trail mix as a donation to keep the world wild. Is my acceptance of being used as a blood-filled canteen related to my feeling that sequoias are never looking down on me? Or that I enjoy eavesdropping on a conversation between a pair of blue jays but feel relieved that I don't have to contribute anything. Or maybe it's that I can make eye contact with a chipmunk, but when he runs off, I never feel rejected."

"Oh, that chipmunk is rejecting you. You're deluding yourself."

"You're right, but rejection by a rodent I can handle."

Henry said, "I enjoyed the woods as a boy, but I was also learning how to make pencils under my father's tutelage."

"You made pencils and wrote classic books. You've cut down more trees than Paul Bunyan."

"It's almost like loving Mother Nature even though she gave me tuberculosis and you ALS."

"I don't blame her. If God really wanted us not to kill, he wouldn't have created a my-dinner-is-your-last-supper planet."

We stood and looked out at the pond. Swimming children were at one end. A kayaker was paddling at the other end. The forest gripped the shore. "A park is where the natural world and people get along," I said.

Henry looked at me. "We have to start thinking of the entire earth as a park."

"When I was a boy," I said, "my father unconsciously and unsuccessfully tried to make me heterosexual by wooing me with Mother Nature. While driving, he would point out deer or woodchucks grazing by the side of the road, which would make me pop up in the backseat, trying to spot—and usually missing—a wild animal. In kindergarten, our family lived from paycheck to paycheck, and my parents would pick me up at school at noon and drive from Buffalo to Batavia to get my dad's salary from the state police. Afterward, he'd drive to the nearby

Bergen-Byron Swamp to show me the thousands of migrating ducks and geese and also entertain me with horror stories about the massasauga rattlesnakes that lived in the spooky-looking marshland. In the summer, he took me fishing where I learned it was okay to kill an earthworm for the thrill of seeing a perch or sunfish for a minute before tossing him back in the river or pond."

"Fishing is a painful lesson about life," said Henry. "Expect a treat and get a hook in your mouth."

"In the sixth grade, I celebrated the first Earth Day in 1970 by picking up litter on the way to school. Our garbage was collected and displayed in the school auditorium, a project no teacher would initiate today due to the reasonable fear that kids would collect junkie needles and used condoms."

Henry said, "I was very optimistic about flower power during that time. It seemed that people were uniting to save our planet, but the greedy resent the environment, since they believe every time a bird chirps, they should hear ka-ching."

He sat down on a stone retaining wall, and I joined him. The temperature was warm but not sweltering. Hiking isn't fun when mosquitoes leave sweaty footprints.

Henry said, "We're constantly brushing up against death in the natural world: a dead minnow on a beach, a snag oak riddled with woodpecker holes, a croaked frog."

"We all end up as roadkill whether we choose the well-worn path or the one less traveled," I said. "Robert Frost was an advocate of the road less traveled as you were. Frost recommended picking the right road, but I believe the more important choice is your walking companions. If you're stuck with dud friends and lovers, you'll soon be jumping off the first bridge you cross. And everyone needs a fun lover, or you'll be building a cabin in your bedroom because you need some 'alone time.' Amusing friends can help make a disease detour an enjoyable journey, even though you've been told you have ALS, and your doctor is convinced you're heading to the cemetery."

"You know, I traveled a good deal in Concord," said Henry. "Do you feel the same about Buffalo?"

"Part of my being a Nature Boy was a reflexive response to growing up in Buffalo during the 1960s. My memories of living in a grimy, industrially polluted environment are easily revived to this day when I visit my mom and stay in the house I grew up in. Buffalo has improved considerably, but I shudder driving through the still-gritty Black Rock neighborhood, where God, our strict teacher, punishes most adults by making them spend their lives sitting in a corner bar. The houses—with their forty-five-year-old soot-covered, frequently avocado-colored aluminum siding—remind me of reading when I was a kid that Lake Erie is dying, even though every summer we swam in it."

"How do you kill a great lake? It's Lilliputians murdering Gulliver."

"Stop!" shouted a blonde girl who looked eight years old. She was being splashed by her younger brother; he looked to be about four. They reminded me of Maddie and Xander.

"We also played in the fields surrounding the nearby Linde plant," I said. "It's now a Superfund site due to radioactive waste dumped from the Manhattan Project. Pheasants lived in the fields, but now I wonder if they weren't mutated sparrows. They don't know what causes ALS, but soldiers have a high rate of the disease, and there's speculation that it might be triggered by stress or environmental factors. It's hard not to dwell on all that running with my friends through fields of plutonium probably wasn't the best way to enjoy the outdoors."

"We were just seeing the dawn of factories when I was young," said Henry. "It's hard to appreciate nature when you're spending your life toiling in a brick coffin."

"Buffalo was filled with elm trees and smokestacks when I was growing up. The elms were enough to make me love nature. Oh, and Charles Burchfield, the painter. He lived in a suburb of Buffalo when I was a kid. Do you know him?"

"We're friends."

"His watercolors are how you experience nature. He's a genius."

"I agree," said Henry. "You must have enjoyed Niagara Falls. It's close to Buffalo."

"Niagara Falls and the Niagara River were my Walden Pond."

"I'm guessing not as swimmable."

"Actually, we did swim above the falls. When I was twelve, I used to go sailing with my friend Fritz. His parents let him use their sailboat. I'm not sure if that would happen now. Parents treat their children like employees who need constant supervision."

"Boys and girls need some autonomy, or else they'll end up hating their bosses."

"There was a huge T-shaped dock that stuck out in the river. You could see the mist from the falls off in the distance. We jumped in the river off the right side of the *T*, and the current was so swift we were whisked to the left side of the *T* in a second. We had to grab the dock's ladder. No life preservers. We could have been swept over the falls but never worried about that."

"Boys play like they're immortal. That's the real definition of childishness. The Angel of Death is still a Halloween costume."

"My grandparents lived in Niagara Falls, and my uncle had a house on the lower Niagara River—right on the gorge. The view made a four-year-old boy gawk. The best thing was there weren't any fences in the yards. There was a deep plummet into the river. I played there after being warned by my grandmother, 'Stay away from the edge. You don't want to drop like a turd.'"

"Did she really say that?"

"Yes. My grandmother had me laughing all the time. She was a country club lady with a blue-collar mouth. They had an apartment that overlooked Goat Island."

Goat Island separates the American Falls from Horseshoe Falls.

"I spent five days in Niagara Falls and botanized on Goat Island," said Henry.

"I never knew until recently that you spent time there. It was like learning Shakespeare went to my high school. Goat Island is a state park that felt like my grandparents' backyard. When I was ten, I would visit them and walk over there. I loved the rushing rapids and calm rabbits. They nibbled the grass and seemed oblivious to the tourists. I also saw my first trilliums in the woods there."

Henry said, "I saw trilliums there, too."

"When I read that, it thrilled me, and it also gave me hope: knowing that a wildflower could survive for over a hundred and fifty years in what's now an urban park."

The islands above the falls and the Niagara Gorge are the home of many rare plants, including old-growth red and white cedars. It's an example of the strange durability of nature in ugly fraternal-twin cities— Niagara Falls, New York, and Niagara Falls, Ontario.

Henry added, "Goat Island is so close to the falls. It seems to be deciding whether to jump or not."

"Actually Henry, I have a comedian friend whose sister killed herself at the falls. When my friend talked about it, every word sounded as if it was written in an excruciating font."

I explained to Henry about my sister Carol's suicide. She shot herself. I was the only family member who lived near her and sat in the hospital waiting room all night while she was kept on life support. Bandaged bullet holes on both sides of her head. Carol had called me three times that day and I tried to get her to come to my house and have dinner with my dear friend Elvira Kurt. She's a brilliant comedian and I knew she would make Carol laugh. Elvira was staying with me. When the Los Angeles's sheriff's office told me the news, I buckled over as if the Grim Reaper had tripped me with his scythe. Elvira offered to cancel her stand-up job the next day. I wouldn't let her bag it since getting a good paying stand-up gig is like seeing a bald eagle or a hummingbird. It might happen again, but you can never predict it. After finishing my story, I said, "Even talking about that is hard."

Henry patted my shoulder. "That sounds excruciating. I'm sorry you had to go through that."

"It was worse than my diagnosis of ALS," I said. "The death of a beloved brother or sister creates a leaky faucet of tears that can never be fixed. It will aggravate and unsettle you for your entire life."

"That's life—being gnawed by a bear while you're enjoying the birds and the bees."

Thoreau's often wrongly depicted as a stern New England crank or oddball, but one story about him reveals how he loved his friends and family with the same passion that he loved nature. When Henry was twenty-five, his brother John, two years older, cut a finger on his left hand while stropping his razor. John was infected with the tetanus bacterium and eleven days later died of lockjaw in Henry's arms. Eleven days after his brother's death, Henry developed the symptoms of lockjaw, a psychosomatic reaction to the loss of his closest friend. As someone whose beloved sister committed suicide, I loved Thoreau even more after reading that heartrending story.

He evidently didn't want to talk about his brother's death. Henry continued to gaze out at the pond, and in the long-established masculine manner of eluding the enemy—an emotion—changed the subject.

"Let's take a walk," suggested Henry. "We'll hike around the pond. I love trails that circumscribe ponds. It gives you a sense of accomplishment without wearing you out."

"Who doesn't enjoy a lazy hike?"

"Just make sure your epitaph isn't 'Here lies a lazy hiker.'"

"Henry, is our life a hike?"

"I think it is. We pick our companions. We're bothered by gnats but enjoy flowers. We're bit by mosquitoes, but love also reminds us our blood is flowing."

"You can pick the wrong trail or get lost."

"Or you can change directions and pick the right path."

"You can scurry like a chipmunk or slink like a snake."

Henry gave me a facetious glance. "Or fuck like a bunny."

I laughed.

Henry said, "There are times you'll feel alone on the trail even when surrounded by friends and family."

"Like when you get a grim diagnosis."

"But you're not alone," said Henry. "We live in a one-room hut called a head. It seems like we live in a wilderness, but we all live at Walden Pond. It seems isolated, but loving companions are just beyond the dark forest of feelings. Once we understand that you have to be hospitable and invite friends and lovers to visit our cabins," Henry pointed to his noggin, "we feel less alone."

"My forest of feelings right now is that I'll die, and the people I love—Michael, Maddie, and Xander and the rest of my family and friends—will be left without forests, prairies, or tundra. The earth will be a parking lot, filled with gas-guzzling hearses because we were too stupid to understand that climate change will mean we can't grow enough food to feed ourselves."

"Bob, you can be lackadaisical or do something to help Mother Nature. Not stopping stupidity means we're not an intelligent species. It's telling that Neanderthals were more ecological than we are. They didn't kill the last wooly mammoths. We did."

"I know. On Wrangel Island in the arctic four thousand years ago."

"Imagine if mammoths still walked the earth."

"You're known for your essay on civil disobedience, but you weren't a pacifist," I said. "You understood that sometimes you have to fight for justice. You defended John Brown by writing that it was okay to kill evil people."

Henry nodded. "I wrote, 'It was his peculiar doctrine that a man has a perfect right to interfere by force with the slaveholder, in order to rescue the slave. I agree with him . . . I do not wish to kill nor to be killed, but I can foresee circumstances in which both these things would be by me unavoidable.'"

"You memorized it," I said, thinking he must have an ego bigger than God's.

"No, I didn't," said Henry. "After writers die, every word they published is embedded in their memories. Depending on your writing skills that's either heaven or hell."

"Your other quote that proves you weren't a pacifist was about the pyramids."

"Yes," he said, "I wasn't a pacifist. 'As for the pyramids, there is nothing to wonder at in them so much as the fact that so many men could be found degraded enough to spend their lives constructing a tomb for some ambitious booby, whom it would have been wiser and manlier to drown in the Nile, and then given his body to the dogs.'"

"We have a bunch of ambitious boobies denying climate change; they're trying to turn the entire earth into a tomb for every species."

"Slavery wouldn't have ended without the deaths of six hundred thousand young Americans."

This wasn't the first time I thought we might have to kill people to save polar bears.

"We have heads of corporations who behave like plantation owners," I said. "They think they own their employees."

"Taking a man's life for murdering a species seems like justice to me. History has a few examples where we had to kill. If the ancient Greeks hadn't fought the Persians, democracy might be a forgotten story. If the British hadn't fought alone against the Nazis, swastikas might be waving over millions of more corpses. Now we're fighting to defend our planet."

I said, "I want my children to fall asleep to 'happily ever after,' not some story about selfish billionaire pigs who inspire every spider on earth to spin webs that say 'Kill them NOW!'"

"E. B. White would love that," said Henry.

"A literary allusion isn't going to save our planet," I said. "During the 1930s, the last surviving ivory-billed woodpeckers lived in the Singer tract of old-growth in Louisiana. The logging company was offered two hundred thousand dollars not to cut down the trees. The company president James F. Griswold said, "We are just money-grubbers. We are not concerned, as are you folks, with ethical considerations." They logged the trees killing the last ivorybills. I've seen films of ivorybills and even in black and white their beauty radiates. Who is that selfish?"

"I hope his eternal afterlife is Promethean. He should be bound to rock and every day an ivorybill pecks out his liver."

I burst out laughing and said, "That's perfect!

Henry laughed too.

We both thought about the imminent war to save our planet.

"What are we going to do?" asked Henry. "Our friend Mother Nature needs our help right now. She's fighting for her life too."

It was a natural comparison. The three of us faced life-threatening conditions. Henry had tuberculosis, I had ALS, and she has to deal with a bunch of greedy people.

"It's a Greek tragedy," said Henry. "We're murdering our mother."

"A comedy might prevent this tragedy. A new *Lysistrata* where trophy wives stop fucking billionaires until they end global warming."

"Inhuman people are afflicted with the curse of Narcissus," said Henry. "They don't care about anyone else because they only love themselves. While they're staring at their reflections in ponds, we should drown the boobies."

"How is it that some people lack empathy?" I asked. "I guess we're lucky. We're writers with life-threatening illnesses. We can imagine other people's lives. I don't want my last words to be "That's mine!"

"It is a bedeviling question that still haunts me," said Henry. "The one lesson my life has taught me is that every heartbeat is a nudge to express love."

"These evil climate change deniers believe they have the right to shoot and kill intruders in their mansions."

"Well, the earth is our home," said Henry. "We have a right to defend it."

"We need a Birnam Wood of Ents!"

"Yes, we do!"

Henry stepped behind a maple tree. I followed—but he was gone. I looked around. A white-breasted nuthatch skittered down the bark of an oak moving like a feathered mouse. The faint scent of pine branch armpits filled the air. The body odor of plants is usually pleasant, which is probably why no rose has ever stopped to sniff a human. The trees were dappled with adorable freckles of light reflected from the water.

It was a shock to see that Henry had departed, but I didn't feel abandoned or alone. He had given me reasons to fight for our world. Henry's not a ghost. His books have made him a true friend to me and the entire planet. As long as children, ducklings, and hotties swim at Walden Pond, Henry lives.

Acknowledgments

I'd like to thank all of my friends for their advice, patience, and enthusiasm: John Bateman, Fred Blair, Chloe Brushwood-Rose, Maggie Cadman, Michael Carroll, Pierre Cousseillant, Judy Gold, Jackie Haught, Elvira Kurt, Idris Larry, Cori Lee, David McConnell, Keith McDermott, Tim Miller, Kevin Pinzone, Patrick Ryan, Eddie Sarfaty, Chris Shirley, Court Stroud, Don Weise, Kathleen Warnock, and Brad Williams.

My sincere gratitude goes to my editor, Raphael Kadushin, and to Sheila Leary, Carla Marolt, Sheila McMahon, Adam Mehring, Amber Rose, and the rest of the wonderful staff at the University of Wisconsin Press.

To my agent and friend, Rob Weisbach, my deepest appreciation for all that he's done to make this book a reality.

I'm forever in debt to my fellow writer Chris Bram for being so generous with his time and talent.

And, I cannot express how important the love, support, and encouragement of my partner, Michael Zam, has been to me throughout this entire project.

LIVING OUT

Gay and Lesbian Autobiographies

David Bergman, Joan Larkin, and Raphael Kadushin
SERIES EDITORS

*The Last Deployment: How a Gay, Hammer-Swinging Twentysomething
Survived a Year in Iraq*
Bronson Lemer

Eminent Maricones: Arenas, Lorca, Puig, and Me
Jaime Manrique

Body Blows: Six Performances
Tim Miller

1001 Beds: Performances, Essays, and Travels
Tim Miller

Cleopatra's Wedding Present: Travels through Syria
Robert Tewdwr Moss

Taboo
Boyer Rickel

Secret Places: My Life in New York and New Guinea
Tobias Schneebaum

Wild Man
Tobias Schneebaum

Sex Talks to Girls: A Memoir
Maureen Seaton

Treehab: Tales from My Natural, Wild Life
Bob Smith

Outbound: Finding a Man, Sailing an Ocean
William Storandt